Caught In the Crossfire:

The Impact of Divorce on Young People

by

LORRAINE HENRICKS, M.D.

THE PIA PRESS

This book is not intended to replace personal medical care and/or professional supervision; there is no substitute for the experience and information that your doctor or mental health professional can provide. Rather, it is our hope that this book will provide additional information to help people understand the impact of divorce on adolescents and the emotional and psychiatric problems that can evolve.

Proper treatment should always be tailored to the individual. If you read something in this book that seems to conflict with your doctor or mental health professional's instructions, contact him/her. There may be sound reasons for recommending treatment that may differ from the information presented in this book.

If you have any questions about any treatment in this book, please consult your doctor or mental health care professional.

In addition, the names and cases used in this book do not represent actual people, but are composite cases drawn from several sources.

All rights reserved
Copyright © 1991 The PIA Press

No part of this book may be reproduced or transmitted
in any form or by any means, electronic or mechanical,
including photocopying, recording, or by any information
storage and retrieval system, without permission in writing from
the publisher.
For information write:
Psychiatric Institutes of America,
part of the National Medical Enterprises Specialty Hospital Group.
1010 Wisconsin Ave. NW
Washington, D.C. 20007

Table of Contents

Preface 1
CHAPTER 1: A Wrenching Experience for
            Everyone.. 5
CHAPTER 2: Divorce for Adults AND Young
            People 20
CHAPTER 3: Understanding Your Children............. 41
CHAPTER 4: Parental Warfare: Roots and
            Remedies 57
CHAPTER 5: The Double Whammy of a Failed
            Marriage and Floundering Kids 76
CHAPTER 6: Getting Help.. 91
CHAPTER 7: Your Changing Relationship 102
SOURCES: 113

DEDICATION

To Hank and Evelyn, my mother and father, whose lives have always been my inspiration.

ACKNOWLEDGMENT

I would like to gratefully acknowledge Peter, Marci, Michael, Tina, Stephanie and Sandy for contributing of themselves to the creation of this book. May their experience provide guidance so that young people are not "Caught In The Crossfire".

Also I would like to gratefully acknowledge Margaret McCaffrey for her considerable skills, insights and contributions to this book.

ABOUT THE AUTHOR

Lorraine Henricks, M.D., is Director of The Foundry, The Young People's Program at Regent Hospital in New York City. She received her Doctor of Medicine degree from the University of Saskatchewan, Canada, did her psychiatric residency at McGill University in Montreal, and completed her fellowship in child and adolescent psychiatry at New York University/Bellevue Medical Center. She is currently a Clinical Professor in the Department of Child and Adolescent Psychiatry at New York University Medical Center. Dr. Henricks is nationally recognized for her work with adolescents and was founder and co-director of The Door, a comprehensive treatment center for adolescents. She has served on numerous committees and task forces and lectures frequently about adolescent mental health and chemical dependency treatment. Dr. Henricks is also author of "Kids Who Do/Kids Who Don't, A Parent's Guide to Teens And Drugs".

Preface

When the Walls Come Tumbling Down

The pain resulting from divorce reverberates through the voices of the patients I see. Susan, a bright, attractive 18-year-old, remembers her parents' divorce, which happened ten years ago.

I remember my parents calling us all into the living room and sitting us down and saying that they didn't love each other any more so they were getting a divorce. I was about 8 years old, and I started to cry. I didn't really know what the word divorce meant, but I knew it wasn't good. My father moved out the next day, and they had to peel me off him. I just remember sitting and crying for days. I was so scared and so angry.

My parents had always fought a lot, and I guess deep down I knew something was wrong. Maybe I was afraid that they would split up. But I just couldn't believe it when it finally happened. I remember thinking that it was somehow my fault. I wasn't the best kid in the world so I thought my father was leaving because I was so bad. My mom said that wasn't true, but it took a long time before I believed her.

It felt so strange not having my father there all of the time. The house seemed empty without him. I hated having to visit him in his apartment. He hardly had any furniture, and he seemed so sad. My mother never said much about it and she seemed real sad, too. Whenever I asked why they got a divorce, she would change the subject. Even today, I don't really understand it.

I kept thinking over and over, Why did this have to happen to me? I played by myself most of the time and just tried to cheer my mother up the best I could. But it wasn't easy because I was sad most of the time myself. And guess I still am.

Fourteen-year-old Sammy, whose parents are in the process of getting a divorce, talks about the experience.

I think my parents are being real jerks about the whole thing. Their marriage isn't that bad. They fight a lot, but it's no worse than a lot of other parents I know. I don't understand why they can't work it out. Our lives are going to be a real mess because of this. My mother has to go back to school so she can get a better job. She's busy and tired all of the time. We never have enough money to do things. We had to sell our summer house which was really a bummer. We always had so much fun there.

My father's seeing this other woman, and I don't think he even really likes her that much. It's all so stupid. It's partly because of his drinking that my mom threw him out. In a way I don't blame her, but I still wish she hadn't done it. It makes everything so weird. Christmas is weird. My birthday is weird because now he's like this visitor. He comes, but he doesn't say much and there's always a fight right before he leaves.

I've been getting into a lot of trouble in school lately. But I just don't care about anything anymore.

Why should I? They don't care about me, so why should I care about them? My life is totally screwed up anyway, so what does it matter what I do?

Agnes, age 37, divorced her husband of eight years when she was 25. Looking back, she recalls:

> I was scared for my sons—they were 5 and 3 then—but I was so hurt and angry with my husband that I guess I didn't protect them much. We fought and screamed all the time, and they would hide under the bed. I remember crying and asking God to forgive me, but I couldn't help it. I prayed that they were tough enough and would get over it someday.
>
> My husband had a girlfriend, and I wanted to kill him for it. He had been lying to me for years, and that drove me crazy. I had no choice but to leave him, but it was the hardest thing I ever did. We had no money so I had to work. I had to leave the boys with babysitters, and I always worried about them.
>
> When they got into school, they weren't doing well, and I felt too exhausted to help them. It was overwhelming. They became so hard to handle, getting into fights, never listening to me. I don't know how I managed really. I was angry at them, too. Why couldn't they behave better? Some kids help their mothers when things get tough. Why couldn't mine? Of course, I blamed their father. They were a lot like him and it scared me.
>
> Now, of course, they're really into trouble—drugs, stealing—and I blame myself.

Jack, age 46, who has just moved out of his home, talks about his failing marriage.

> You read all the time about how people change and drift apart, but you never really believe it can happen to you. Nancy and I had a good marriage at

one time, but we've just been going in different directions for too long.

I met somebody who really understands me and I want to be with her. How can I stay with Nancy if I feel that way? And she doesn't really want me to anyway. If we didn't have kids it would be a different story. We both love our children and don't want to hurt them, but we just can't seem to help doing that. We try not to fight in front of them, but they've known for a long time that something is up.

We have two daughters in junior high and a son who is a senior. They're all good kids, but they've all been having problems since we told them we were going to split up. My son and I used to have a great relationship, but now he's all clammed up. He's real quiet and moody now. He won't tell me anything. I'm so scared he's going to start doing drugs or something that I can't sleep at night.

My daughters used to be straight-A students, but both of their marks have dropped. There's a history of mental illness in my wife's family, and I worry about our youngest daughter. She's always been a little skittish and just doesn't seem right these days.

I feel so helpless. I know this is going to hurt them, but what can I do? It makes me feel like such a failure to let them down like this. I know I'm diminished in their eyes, and that hurts.

Chapter 1

A Wrenching Experience for Everyone

Divorce...once a whispered word, something that only happened to *other* people, to movie stars or that family down the street, is now an everyday occurrence that is changing the face of our society.

We've all heard the statistics. One out of every two—some experts say even as many as two out of three—first marriages are going to end in divorce. Second marriages have an even bleaker prospect of succeeding. An estimated 40 percent of American children now come from broken homes. If current trends continue the Stepfamily Association of America projects that by the twenty-first century there will be more step or re-formed families in this country than natural ones.

Though in the past divorce was always assumed to be hard on children, some might feel that its prevalence today somehow alleviates the damage. Since *everyone* seems to be doing it, shouldn't that make it less traumatic?

In my more than twenty years as a psychiatrist working with troubled adolescents and young adults, I can tell you that, sadly, this is not so. Even though divorce is becoming the norm in our society, as you can see from the examples cited in the Preface, it is still a wrenching experience that usually causes much heartache and stress for all involved.

It is estimated that children from divorced families make up 60 percent of children in clinical treatment and 80 percent of adolescents in inpatient psychiatric treatment programs. They often turn to drugs or alcohol to soften the pain of their hurt, and frequently have problems in school or with the law. Many become depressed and in extreme cases attempt suicide in a desperate plea for help. Sometimes children of divorce grow up having difficulty forming lasting relationships or get into relationships that repeat the unhealthy patterns of their parents' marriage.

SOMETIMES IT'S THE ONLY SOLUTION

Let me say at the outset, that although divorce is almost always a painful and wrenching experience, sometimes it is the only solution to an impossibly bad marriage.

Though you should avoid it if at all possible, that doesn't mean you should do so at all costs. Staying in an unhappy marriage where profound differences are never resolved has a corrosive effect on both parents and children that is comparable to that of divorce itself.

But before you do take the plunge, knowing just what you are getting into can make the difference between sinking or swimming. Therefore it is my goal to help you navigate through the stormy waters of divorce so that you and your children can make it safely to the next shore in as good a shape as possible.

If you are currently floundering in any of the different stages of divorce, being aware of what you are going through or have been through can be the first crucial step in avoiding or undoing a whole host of hurtful mistakes.

PICTURE NOT ENTIRELY BLEAK

But this is not *always* the case. While many children of divorce are hurt and remain so for many years, a large proportion grow up stronger and wiser for the experience. Therefore, one of my main purposes in this book will be to show you the many things you can do to lessen the negative impact of divorce on your teens and young adults, and to help them use the experience to grow in their understanding.

ONE OF LIFE'S GREATEST STRESSORS

Some researchers feel that divorce, right along with death of a spouse, is *the* most stressful life experience that an individual can have, and I would have to agree. Just as with the death of one's partner, in divorce an individual's whole life changes dramatically. No matter how bad the marriage might have been, deeply rooted emotional, attitudinal, and behavioral habits have been developed in the relationship that both partners come to depend on for their identity and sources of strength. When the couple decides to divorce, these habits are torn from their roots and must be replaced with new ones, which is no easy task.

HARD ON PARENTS

Husbands usually move out of their homes and set up housekeeping for themselves. Trying to support two households instead of one puts them under enormous financial strain. Where once they were the powerful male figure in the home and to their children, they suddenly become sometime visitors and part-time fathers, a diminishment in status that can undermine self-esteem and leave many feeling shame and embarrassment. Indeed, divorce has been found, not surprisingly, to be one of the most common stressors leading to depression in white middle-class adult males in this country.

Women, on the other hand, are usually left alone to fend for themselves as single parents. Their incomes usually drop drastically, with financial concerns becoming a drain on their time and energy. Those who didn't work previously must scramble for some way to earn a living. Those who do work already often must increase their hours, and become exhausted by the dual demands of work and parenting singlehandedly. It's no wonder that women often feel depressed and overwhelmed under these circumstances.

MAYBE EVEN MORE DIFFICULT THAN DEATH OF A SPOUSE

Though many of these same changes also occur when a spouse dies, there are important differences. When one's partner dies, it is certainly a terrible blow. But there is usually much support from friends and community, which is often totally lacking in divorce. When a spouse dies, there is also a natural mourning process which adults and children go through and which helps them to heal from their loss. The very finality of death also helps people to close one chapter and get on with rebuilding their lives.

In divorce there is grieving as well, but it is interfered with by the fact that the other person is still very much alive. Children, especially, often cling to the hope that their parents will someday reunite.

THE HURT GOES ON FOR YEARS

When there are children involved, former spouses usually continue to be very much a part of each other's lives. Unfortunately, they often go on hurting each other for years. The legacy of their bad relationship lives on as they negotiate parental visitation, financial support, how to spend holidays, remarriage, and important rituals in their children's lives, such as birthdays, graduation, marriage, and the birth of grandchildren. In many cases, the wound just never heals.

MOST PEOPLE UNPREPARED

In my experience, most people are totally unprepared for the emotional and financial toll a divorce takes and for the problems that can result for themselves and for their children. Because they go through it in the dark, with few road maps or signposts to guide them, they inevitably get lost in the alien territory into which they are embarking.

CHILDREN INEVITABLY WOUNDED IN THE CROSSFIRE

Most couples get so caught up in their own pain that they can't see the damage their anger and fighting are doing to the young and innocent in their midst.

Though, as I pointed out earlier, divorce is extremely stressful for adults, it is even more so for children. Just by virtue of their immaturity and complete dependence on their parents, young people are terribly vulnerable to the turmoil that divorce inevitably brings. As we saw in the examples mentioned in the Preface, their whole world falls apart and they feel helpless, angry, and confused.

Before parents realize what is happening, they not only have a troubled marriage, but troubled children as well. Parents then feel so guilty that they often can't do what is necessary to get their children the proper help.

DON'T BLAME YOURSELF

From the outset, let me say that most of the parents I have worked with love their children and don't want to hurt them. The problem is that divorce is such a traumatic, overwhelming experience for them that they unwittingly hurt their offspring in the process. Though as adults, we must take responsibility for our behavior and the effect it has on others, in this case endless self-blaming is counterproductive.

If you have been through a divorce, you have, as I pointed out earlier, been through one of the greatest life stressors there is. Most of us aren't at our best during a crisis, and you should not blame yourself unduly if you have done things and behaved in ways that you regret, even in regard to your children.

The important thing is to try to be objective: to see what's really going on with yourself *and* especially with your sons and daughters. You can't erase the past, but you can learn from it. You can't undo your mistakes, but you can learn how to be better parents from this point on. By doing so, you can make a big difference in helping your teens or young adults to grow up healthy and happy, and to have successful marriages of their own.

If you are in the process of a divorce now or are contemplating one, you have the advantage of being able to alter your behavior in a positive manner before damage is done. In this way you can prevent an enormous amount of pain for yourself and your children.

AMBIVALENCE NORMAL

Though most people do love their children, it is also true that many of us also feel ambivalence toward our offspring. Maybe you were so young when you had them that you feel cheated out of your own childhood. Maybe having children has squeezed you financially or leaves you more exhausted than you ever anticipated. Or perhaps you have a child with special problems or a difficult personality who has taxed you beyond your limit. Those who did not receive adequate love and nurturing from their own parents are particularly prone to experiencing ambivalence toward their children.

I sometimes encounter couples who believe that their marriage has deteriorated since the birth of their children because of all the strains parenting places on them. They have less time to be alone together, less time and money for fun and frivolity. Sometimes they blame the children outright for the breakdown of the marriage.

Though some ambivalence is normal especially during the stress of a divorce, in its extremes it can do real damage to young people. It is important for you to be aware of your mixed feelings about your children and to not torture yourself with guilt about them. But, as I will discuss in later chapters, it is equally vital for their well-being that you do not burden their impressionable minds and emotions with your resentments and doubts about them.

DIVORCE: A RECENT BUT UNIVERSAL PHENOMENON

Though divorce has existed for a long time, the increase in marital breakups in the past few decades is truly phenomenal. The divorce rate doubled between 1970 and 1981; in 1981 the number of divorces was three times what it had been in 1962. Even though there has been some leveling off of that rate in the past few years, some researchers feel that it is too soon to predict any reversal in trends. Most agree that the effects divorce has already had on our society are profound and sure to be long-lasting.

Fortunately, because we live in the era of the social sciences, during the past two decades divorce has been intensely studied and analyzed. Psychologists, sociologists, and psychiatrists such as myself have been looking at this problem from a variety of perspectives in an effort to understand its many dimensions.

Scientific studies have confirmed, for example, that divorce does have profound effects on children that often last for many years. Though individual circumstances may be very different, these effects and the process of divorce itself is similar for everyone, no matter what their socioeconomic status, their race, or their religion. We have also learned that there are healthy and unhealthy ways for parents to handle their divorce.

This kind of information gives people who are divorcing today an enormous advantage over those who went through divorce even a few years ago. By looking at the mistakes of other parents, you can learn specific ways to minimize the pain and heartache for everyone.

One of the main purposes of this book, therefore, is to help you to benefit from the knowledge gained through this research and through my experience as a practitioner working with troubled teens, young adults, and families.

CAUSES OF DIVORCE

Some people like to blame our loosening mores and recent sexual revolution as the cause for the increase in divorce. However, most social scientists feel that the problem is much more complex than that. Industrialization, urbanization, changing expectations about what marriage should provide each partner, women's liberation, and economic recessions are all considered to have played a part in the increased breakdown of the family that we are now experiencing.

In addition to these societal pressures, we have come to realize that there are a number of specific issues within marriage that tend to contribute to failure. Financial difficulties, or different styles of spending and saving money are among the most frequently cited causes of divorce. Different parenting approaches, sexual incompatibility, and infidelity also rank high as trigger points for marital breakdown.

CHEMICAL DEPENDENCY A MAJOR FACTOR

In my experience, chemical dependency of one partner is also a frequent contributor to serious problems in marriage. Along with mood disorders, chemical dependency is considered to be the major psychiatric disorder of the decade; it is said to affect between 10 to 15 percent of the population. As one partner advances in the stages of chemical dependency, the marriage inevitably becomes strained.

Because of its pervasive effect on a person's behavior, chemical dependency involves many of those pressure points in a marriage mentioned earlier that threaten its very stability. Reckless spending habits, diminished parenting ability, problems in sexual performance, and an increased tendency toward infidelity are all hallmarks of chemical dependency. Obviously, this places an enormous stress on any relationship, and understandably often leads to its rupture.

By the same token, the stress of divorce can push vulnerable individuals, both children and parents alike, into bad habits or intensify already existing ones. When the tension mounts, a drink or some mood-altering drug all too often becomes the routine remedy for easing the pain. A link between drug and alcohol use in children of divorce has been found in a number of studies. Preliminary data from an ongoing survey at The Regent Hospital, to date including 203 patients, suggests that those persons from broken homes were approximately 1.5 times more likely to have parents with a history of drug use than those from intact families.

DEPRESSION ALSO CONTRIBUTES

Depression is the leading psychiatric disorder of our times, currently affecting some 20 percent of the population. As with chemical dependency, depression both contributes to and is exacerbated by the breakdown of marriage. Its debilitating effects ripple through a family, often drowning other members in their wake. Data from that same survey of our population at The Regent Hospital also suggest that 12.5% more patients from divorced families exhibited depressive symptoms than those from intact families.

CHEMICAL DEPENDENCY, DEPRESSION, AND DIVORCE LINKED

As you can see, chemical dependency, depression, and divorce are not only prevalent, but they are also linked in significant ways. Both disorders can cause and be the result of divorce for all family members. Moreover, depression often leads to chemical dependency and vice versa, so that many individuals suffer from both at the same time.

Consequently, a main thrust of this book will be to help you understand these disorders and their interrelationships with divorce.

OTHER REASONS

Of course there are many other reasons that people get divorced. Violence, incest, homosexuality, mental illness, and criminal behavior are among the most extreme. At the other end of the spectrum are such comparatively mild factors as partners drifting apart over the years or realizing that they just don't have that much in common after all.

DIVORCE'S EFFECTS ON CHILDREN

One of the basic demands of parenting is that of self-sacrifice. To be a parent means to give up large amounts of your time and energy for the raising of your children. Even under normal circumstances, most of us feel stretched to our limits by this responsibility.

When couples are in the throes of a divorce, in a sense they often regress and become like children again themselves. They are so angry and hurt that the normal "adult" practice of restraint and consideration for others disappears. Instead, they can turn into bickering, name-calling brawlers with little regard for those around them. Thinking only of themselves, parents can turn into self-absorbed children who lose all perspective about the effects their behavior can have on the very ones they are charged with protecting.

One of my aims is to help you put aside your own pain and needs for a while and to step back into your role of parent again. This will mean trying to look at the divorce experience through the eyes of your teens or young adults, for only then can you fully appreciate their plight and learn how to alleviate it.

CHILDREN NOT "LITTLE ADULTS"

One of the hardest concepts for many parents to grasp is the idea that children are not just "little adults." Somehow, time and distance makes us forget what it's like to be small, helpless, and totally dependent. Even though we know that children are still developing emotionally and mentally, we often act as though we assume that they are much more mature than their age or developmental level would warrant. This is truer today than ever, as children are rushed to grow up quickly, giving the impression in their language and dress of being sophisticated beyond their years. And, of course, it is especially true for teens and young adults who are close to maturity but in many crucial ways are still dependent on their parents.

As I noted previously, being a parent is not easy, even under the best of circumstances. Children aren't that simple to understand, and it is the exceptional parent who has the talent to interpret correctly everything his or her teens or young adults do, and to give the "best" or most helpful response. During divorce your parenting abilities diminish greatly. If you are baffled and worry that you have made mistakes, don't feel inadequate or hopeless. There is a whole field of psychology devoted to understanding children and their different developmental stages. I'm going to share some of that knowledge with you because I believe it will enable you to help your teens and young adults through the divorce experience.

DIVORCE CAN PRECIPITATE PROBLEMS IN VULNERABLE YOUNG PEOPLE

I want to point out from the outset that though divorce is a major stressor, it is not the cause of problems in young people. By this I mean that divorce in itself does not necessarily cause emotional breakdowns. Current thinking in psychiatry and medicine tells us that we are all born with certain strengths and weaknesses, mental and physical. If we have weaknesses in one area, this predisposes us to certain illnesses if we are under stress of any kind.

We know that certain psychological problems, for instance, run in families, and we therefore assume that they have a genetic basis. People born into families in which there is a history of chemical dependency or mental illness have a biological predisposition to these conditions that could be triggered by a number of life stresses. Divorce is certainly one of them, but so is the death of a parent or having one or both parents with either of these diseases. By the same token, poverty or major catastrophes, such as an earthquake or a serious accident, can all lead to breakdown in vulnerable individuals.

PROBLEMS PRECIPITATED BY DIVORCE

Teens or young adults can react to the stress of their parents' divorce with a broad variety of disorders. Some of them might overlap, with some individuals exhibiting two or more at any one time. These behaviors might not be serious and could disappear over time. But when they become extreme, and continue for more than a few months, they might signal the early stages of disease processes, such as chemical dependency, depression, or eating disorders or other psychiatric disorders. In Chapter Five, I will go into detail about the following behaviors: how you can tell when they are serious and what you should do about them. I will also describe specific psychiatric disorders and how you can recognize them.

COMMON WAYS CHILDREN REACT TO DIVORCE

Behavior problems such as aggressiveness, argumentativeness, drug taking or alcohol abuse, breaking the law, pranks, uncooperativeness, promiscuity, staying out late at night, running away.
Withdrawal from activity. Uncommunicativeness, sadness, breaking off with friends, and so on.
School problems, drop in grades, truancy.
Somatic complaints such as headaches, stomachaches, and so on.
Marked changes in eating habits, such as compulsive eating or not eating.

PURPOSES OF THIS BOOK

As I stated earlier, one of the main purposes of this book is to make you aware of the potential effects divorce can have on your teens and young adults. In order to do this, I will focus on the different phases of divorce, the stresses each phase brings, and how you can lessen those stresses. I will also discuss the different developmental stages of teens and young adults to help you better understand them.

The different problems that young people can experience when their parents divorce, summarized above, will be analyzed in great depth so that you can recognize warning signs and take preventive measures. I will also provide pointers on how to get help if your teen or young adult is already in the throes of serious emotional or behavioral difficulties.

GETTING HELP WHEN YOU NEED IT

Though today there is much counseling and therapy available for couples in trouble, in our society there is still resistance to getting help. Perhaps it's a rugged individualist mentality that prevents us from turning to others when we are in need. Perhaps it is the shame that many still feel at having a failed marriage. Whatever the reason, the majority of people go through a divorce on their own. And this is most unfortunate.

As a psychiatrist, I can tell you that getting help for yourself as a couple early on in the divorce process can make a tremendous difference in how stressful the process becomes for you and your children. By the same token, individual counseling for different family members is often the key to avoiding serious problems down the road.

This is my conclusion after more than twenty years of experience in this field. As a result, I will make specific suggestions at the end of this book on when and how you should select a therapist or even inpatient treatment for members of your family.

YOUR CHANGING RELATIONSHIP

Finally, whether you remain a single parent or remarry, your relationship with your children after divorce inevitably alters. Consequently in the final chapter I'm going to discuss some of the things you can do to make your new family structure work for you.

Chapter 2

Divorce for Adults *and* Young People

Divorce doesn't play favorites. Regardless of an adult's race, age, or socioeconomic status, the stages of most divorces tend to be remarkably similar. Knowing these stages, an adult can prepare for potential emotional, financial and even psychological pitfalls that are so closely associated with divorce. In fact, most adults have the experience to form at least a basic conception of how divorce will change their lives. Conversely, children lack this experience and subsequently have no realistic expectations of how divorce will change their lives.

In this chapter I will review the stages of divorce: first, from the adults' point of view, then from the children's. My goal is to help you to understand how each stage affects both adults and children. Showing you the same stage from your children's point of view is part of my ongoing effort to give the perspective from their young minds and emotions so that you can be a more perceptive parent.

Keep in mind that the stages of divorce are not absolute and may be assigned different names and time frames by other specialists. I'm describing them in what I think will be the simplest and most helpful fashion. If your experience does not jibe with them exactly or you have read of different stages in another source, remember they are just guidelines to help you make sense out of the chaos of your divorce.

EARLY DISINTEGRATION PHASE

From the Parents' Perspective

Marcia, a 40-year-old teacher, looks back with sadness at the time her marriage started to come undone:

> It was really awful how bitter our fights got. We could barely be in the same room without snarling at each other. The worst part for me was the uncertainty. Were we going to stay together or weren't we? I had such mixed feelings that I couldn't sleep. I didn't think we should or really could make it as a couple anymore, but the thought of being on my own was terrifying.

This is the time when real trouble starts brewing in a relationship. Perhaps there have been problems for years—arguments over money, one partner in some stage of chemical dependency, one partner having a sexual affair, general disagreement over how to handle the kids, distancing and lack of affection between you and your spouse, and so on.

But what often differentiates this stage from the earlier pre-divorce state of the marriage is the escalating intensity of feelings and behavior. Frequently the arguing and hostility start to boil over into everyday exchanges. Even when emotions are suppressed, they tend to come out in subtle but equally potent forms. Sniping and nonverbal communications, such as angry looks and sighs of exasperation, can be just as lethal as out-and-out warfare.

Stress for Both Partners

When a marriage reaches this point, both you and your partner are under considerable stress. Constant discord puts each of you on the defensive. As I noted earlier, even the worst of marriages provides a sense of security to those in it. When there is even a hint that the relationship is in real danger, spouses can feel threatened to their cores. Self-esteem becomes undermined. Fears about the future start to take root. The anger and tension alone take an enormous toll on your emotional and psychological well-being.

During this phase you and your partner both may show drastic changes in mood and behavior. Depression, increased substance abuse if that is an issue, staying away from home for long periods, poor work performance both on the job and in domestic responsibilities, are all common when a marriage starts to really fall apart.

Children's Needs Fall to Second Place

Obviously when under such duress, it's easy to see how your children's needs can be squeezed into second place behind your own. Even if you consciously struggle to protect them, you may still find your ability to nurture and comfort your young ones greatly diminished at this time.

One Partner Initiator

In her book *Uncoupling,* based on a study of separating couples, sociologist Diane Vaughan reports that there tends to be one partner who is the initiator in the breaking up of any relationship. This is the person who first realizes that the marriage is in serious trouble. Though this is not always the case, I do encounter it frequently in my practice. When it occurs, in my experience initiators often communicate this realization by expressing dissatisfaction with their partners in an attempt to get them to change annoying habits or offensive ways of acting. Whether this is successful or not, initiators still often subconsciously or covertly start separating psychologically from their marriages. They do this because deep down they suspect that the marriage cannot be saved.

Secretiveness and Denial Reign

The damaging aspect of this tendency is that openness and honesty about problems are exchanged for secretiveness and denial. Because the possible ending of the marriage is upsetting and threatening to initiators, they put off dealing with it up front. Instead they work through their ambivalence secretly on their own, often creating a separate identity and social life for years before actually sharing the true depth of their dissatisfaction with their partner.

Their partners, too, engage in denial. They are aware that things are not right in the marriage, but they want it to go on at all costs. They don't want to see and can't really believe that things are that bad.

Though the relationship may be progressively deteriorating for years with the initiator pulling farther and farther away, a kind of collusion sets in between the two. Both have a vested interest in pretending that everything is really all right. Initiators essentially just don't have the nerve to bring things out in the open. Even though the signals would be obvious to an outside observer, partners are so blinded by their closeness to the situation and their own denial that they can be totally surprised when serious talk of a divorce actually occurs.

Damaging for Both Partners

Initiators clearly have the advantage, but both partners suffer considerably in such a stifled, dishonest relationship. It takes an enormous amount of psychic energy for initiators to carry on what amounts to a major deception. They are wrestling with all kinds of fears and uncertainties about themselves and their lives that they are not sharing with the person with whom they share their lives. At the same time, they may be involved in ongoing battles with that person in which they never express their true feelings: that is, that the marriage is doomed. In between skirmishes they might even go through the motions of a good relationship, with displays of affection and other reassuring acts that keep their partners off balance.

The other partner, on the other hand, has been placed in a precarious position. He or she is being criticized or is the brunt of dissatisfaction without clearly knowing what is going on. This, plus the energy it takes for them to deny there are problems, puts them in a constant state of tension.

It's easy to see how wrestling with such intense undercurrents in a relationship as described above can leave you and your partner too exhausted to be good parents.

EARLY DISINTEGRATION PHASE

From the Children's Perspective

Nineteen-year-old Tim remembers the days right before his parents separated:

> They had always fought a lot, but there was something different about their arguments that started to scare me. I could tell my mom had had it with him just by the way she put him down, like he was some kind of dope or something. He was still being real sweet to her, as if that could make everything all right. Sometimes she seemed like she was softening up, and I would get my hopes up. But then things would go back to being bad again. I wasn't even sure what divorce was and nobody ever really explained it. But I knew I was in for something pretty awful. I couldn't do my schoolwork and I started getting into trouble. Pretty soon they were both getting on my back, too.

Again, though problems may have been going on for years between you and your partner, your children often sense when things have entered a new, more ominous phase. As I will discuss in greater depth later, children are tuned into their parents' emotions and subconscious thoughts. Consequently, even if the word *divorce* is never mentioned or is only talked about indirectly, young people frequently know that something serious is afoot.

Secrecy and Ambivalence Hard on Children

The secrecy and ambivalence that tends to characterize this phase create a state of emotional confusion and turmoil in your children that is similar to your own. Young people have a hard time expressing themselves directly even under normal circumstances. If they are getting mixed signals and don't know what's really going on, as is usually true at this stage, they tend to express their confusion behaviorally. We call this behavioral expression of emotional states *acting out*, and I will discuss it in depth in a later chapter.

Parental Warfare

Parental warfare is widely considered to be very hard on children, in both intact and divorced families. Chronic fighting and hostility can leave indelible marks on the psyches of young people that often follow them through life and affect their emotional state and behavior for years. They often feel angry, confused, and greatly saddened by what they are witnessing. They fear for themselves and their parents, and they worry about the future. And they almost always feel helpless in the face of so much discord. Since warfare between you and your spouse usually intensifies in this early dissolution phase, it is a particularly stressful time for your teens and young adults.

As I noted above, your and your spouse's behavior often changes radically at this time and your parenting ability greatly diminishes as a result. Just when your children need you the most, you are unavailable to them.

Even if you try to be with them and reassure them, they sense your preoccupation and self-absorption. A scenario that many young people face in this early phase is that of their mothers becoming depressed and their fathers not coming home regularly. No wonder many of them feel lonely and abandoned.

In this early stage of a marriage's dissolution children frequently feel compelled to take sides, which often places them in a state of deep conflict. Often they are so consumed with worry about their parents that they are unable to attend to their own developmental needs. Instead of being with friends and testing their independence from you, they often retreat from peer relationships and take on a parenting role with whichever parent they perceive as being the underdog.

Partners Put Each Other Down

Your anger can be so intense at your partner that you might find yourself complaining about him or her to your teen or young adult. This is common and is one of the most damaging practices of divorcing couples. Almost across the board, the young people I work with complain how much they hate it when one parent puts the other down. On a deep level it causes them much anguish. No matter how badly parents behave, children still identify with them and incorporate aspects of them into their own sense of themselves. When you put down your partner, you are in a real sense putting down your child as well. This is a practice that often continues through all stages of the divorce process and one that should be nipped in the bud early on.

IMPORTANCE OF GETTING HELP IN THIS PHASE

Getting marital counseling in this phase can do much to avert real damage to yourself and your children. The secrecy and ambivalence are hurtful to you and your spouse in that it keeps you from dealing honestly with the issues that are pushing you apart. Counseling at this time can help you to work out your differences in more positive, less destructive ways than you are likely to do on your own.

A qualified counselor can give you real strategies for avoiding the out-and-out conflict that often characterizes this and every phase of a divorce. Many people are even able to prevent a divorce if they get help early on in the process. Even if you are dead set against reconciling with your partner, you can benefit greatly from handling your separation in a less stressful manner.

Your children suffer considerably from the mixed messages and chaos of this period. I can't stress enough how much better it can be for them if you deal with things openly and honestly and in a less hostile atmosphere. Family therapy or even individual therapy for your teens or young adults at this phase of the divorce process could make all the difference in how well they handle your marital problems at the present time as well as for years to come.

OVERT CRISIS PHASE

From Parents' Perspective

To 50-year-old Bob, an advertising executive, the first days of his separation were the worst part of the divorce:

> I couldn't believe it was all really happening. We had been together so long. I kept thinking, How can she do this to me? How can I possibly get along without her? No matter how bad it had been, I would have rather stayed with her than split up. When I finally moved out, it was like I was drugged or something. I could barely put one foot in front of the other.

Here I was after so many years paying for a house, taking care of everything, living in some sterile apartment like a bachelor. I was really a mess for a long time.

This is the time when the fact that you and your spouse are going to separate first comes out into the open. If you are the initiator, you might feel relief that what you have been thinking and feeling for so long is finally becoming a reality. But you could also feel guilt, remorse and fear. Because you might believe that you were forced into a breakup as a result of your partner's behavior, you can also experience much anger, resentment, and ambivalence.

If you are the other partner, as I noted earlier, you might be completely surprised that divorce is imminent. As the person being rejected, you are likely to feel hurt, angry, scared, and confused. You and your partner also might experience panic and intense fear about the gravity of your situation.

Painful Time for All

Overall, this is an extremely painful time for you and your spouse. One partner usually moves out, and this results in a drastic change in your lives and profound sense of loss for both. Acute grief frequently sets in. Having your marital problems out in the open for the first time also can make you feel a sense of shame, failure, and embarrassment.

Fear for Your Children

You are likely to be deeply worried about the effects the divorce will have or is already having on your children. Guilt, plus feelings of helplessness and inadequacy, add to your emotional burden at this time.

External and Internal Changes

Along with these intense internal changes, there are usually extreme external ones as well. As I noted, one person moving out drastically alters everyone's life. The emotional crisis is often accompanied by a financial one that puts a major strain on both you and your partner. In many cases, the woman has to return to work and/or school or increase her hours at the job to make ends meet. The husband feels great pressure at having to maintain two households. The support of friends and community may also disappear as people take sides or turn their backs on you in your struggle.

Most people experience this phase as a nightmare. It's much like the period after an earthquake. Your whole world has crumbled and you are devastated. Even though you are in a state of shock, you must go on and somehow try to rebuild a new life out of the rubble.

OVERT CRISIS PHASE

From the Children's Perspective

Marleen, a stylishly dressed 21-year-old college senior, recalls the first few months of her parent's separation eight years ago:

> I was almost completely paralyzed by the whole thing. Not having Daddy around was awful, and seeing my mother with her new boyfriend was just too painful to bear. Then after a few months I decided to go live with my dad, but that was even worse. He lived in a different part of the state, so I had to leave all of my friends and everything. It was like a bad dream, living in this strange place just with my dad, seeing him so unhappy. Our lives used to be so nice, and now they were so weird. I didn't know who I was anymore, and I started to wish I was dead.

Having their worst fears become a reality is crushing for most children. Though your teens and young adults no doubt knew for some time that things were not right between you and your spouse, they probably hoped desperately that somehow you would stay together.

Childrens' Whole World Falls Apart

Children of all ages instinctively know how dependent they are on their parents. They rely on a stable, secure home life for their proper development and growth. That is one of the reasons that divorce is such a trauma for them. In a real sense, it makes them fear for their very survival.

No matter how bad your relationship with your spouse has been, your children view both of you as important givens in their lives. It's hard for them even to see you as separate individuals sometimes, so the thought of you actually separating can be incomprehensible. Because of this they may deny the seriousness of your problems and be genuinely shocked when they are told that you plan to divorce.

When it actually happens, they feel bewildered, angry, and helpless. Teens and young adults particularly often feel let down by their parents for putting their own needs before theirs. "Why couldn't they work it out?" and "Things weren't that bad" are comments I frequently hear from young people at this stage.

Great Sense of Loss

Teens and young adults also experience a devastating sense of loss. They know that life will never be the same for them. Their home, their family life, and their sense of security have been pulled out from under them. They grieve for an idealized past. Since fathers frequently leave their lives and from then on are only involved with them in a peripheral way, they grieve the loss of this important parent.

Younger adolescents often feel that they are the ones being rejected and may even believe that they were the cause of the breakup. Young adults, on the other hand, often react with great fury at the parent whom they perceive to be the responsible one. Though children this age rarely blame themselves, they often agonize over the belief that they could have somehow done something to prevent the divorce.

An Earthquake Has Hit

Just as this overt crisis phase seems like an earthquake for you, it represents a total collapse of your children's world, too. Many people sell their homes or change apartments in the first year after divorce. Children not only have to adjust to drastic alterations in their family and emotional lives, but have to make new friends at a new school as well. They also can feel shame and embarrassment at their new status. At times this inhibits them with other young people and forces them into isolation just when they need companionship the most.

Feel Abandoned

Since, as I noted above, your parenting ability is seriously compromised in this phase, your children can feel a real sense of abandonment. Cut off from you and their friends, with no one to turn to, vulnerable teens and young adults will often succumb to serious emotional or behavioral problems at this time.

Getting Help Crucial for Children

If you haven't done so previously, getting your teens or young adults into counseling or therapy at this time can be crucial for them. Your separation and imminent divorce is a crisis of major proportions for your children at a time when they are particularly vulnerable.

In the years of adolescence to early adulthood, young people desperately need a stable, consistent environment for proper development. When that is shattered, having an outside person to talk to can provide the support they need to prevent serious problems. Though there are many children who adjust to their parents' divorce without getting outside help, vulnerable individuals almost always do poorly. In a later chapter I will discuss the warning signs that you should look for to know when your teen or young adult is heading for trouble.

Counseling Helpful for You, Too

Also, by being in counseling yourselves at this time, you and your spouse can do much to defuse the tension in your relationship. Since parental warfare is so destructive to children, getting help to handle things in a more peaceful fashion is of utmost importance. Experienced counselors can also help you to navigate through your own emotional and psychological upheavals, which are considerable at this time.

Family and/or individual counseling for both you and your spouse can provide you with much-needed support and guidance that will make your own adjustment much easier. All family members have deep feelings of loss that need to be expressed and dealt with. Even if things can never be patched up, you will remain a family forever. Working things through in a supportive manner can make your continued involvement with each other manageable and even positive for years to come.

THE IMMEDIATE AFTERMATH PHASE

From Parents' Perspective

Forty-two-year-old Liz, a tax accountant, thinks she went through a real identity crisis in the first few years after her divorce:

> The first couple of months actually weren't that bad. In some ways it was a relief to finally do something and get moving on with a new life. But nothing prepared me for how hard it would be to be single again. I guess I had always felt secure about my

attractiveness, but my self-esteem took a beating when I realized a lot of men out there are just interested in sex. It really is true that the pickings are lousy for women over 30. And I had no idea really how exhausting, draining, and overwhelming being a single parent could be. I realized my potential earnings were not as good as I had thought. I learned real fast that I wasn't superwoman, and that hurt my pride more than I can say.

This phase usually lasts three to five years, and occurs when the actual divorce is made final. It is the time when the reality of the divorce actually sets in. Emotions can either have cooled down a bit or are continuing at a high pitch as you and your spouse adjust to new living arrangements and negotiate your new relationship. All kinds of things must still be worked out, and this takes a good deal of energy on both of your parts. If hostility continues, it serves to exacerbate the stress of this already difficult time.

Period of Major Adjustment

If you are the initiator, you may feel happy and relieved that the marriage is over. You may find your new life exciting and a big improvement. On the other hand, you may be disappointed that things are worse than they were in the past. You may feel lonely, depressed, and scared about the future.

If you are the other partner, you still may be struggling with feelings of rejection and unworthiness. You may hold out the hope for a reconciliation and as a result feel unable to start rebuilding a new life.

Being Single Not Easy

Suddenly being single again often proves extremely unsettling for both men and women. After even a few years of being part of a couple, the prospect of dating and starting a new relationship makes almost everyone feel insecure. Rather than risk a new involvement, many turn to their children for comfort, which often turns out to be unhealthy for both the young people and themselves.

New Relationships a New Stress

Even if you have embarked on a new relationship, you are likely to find it fraught with unexpected difficulties. Your failing marriage stays in your life and can infect even a new love with bad memories or ongoing battles. Your children may resent the person you are excited about and who is bringing you happiness. You may feel angry at your teens or young adults if they show their resentment openly and make this person so uncomfortable that it threatens your relationship with him or her.

For people who remarry, having children from a former marriage places all kinds of stresses on the marriage. If the children are having problems of their own, you can feel yourself pulled in different directions, sometimes to the point of breaking.

Changed Parenting Roles Difficult

If you have custody of your children, you may feel overwhelmed as a single parent. No matter how limited your partner's involvement, just having another authority figure around to back you up is significant when trying to raise children. If your partner was a very involved parent, his or her absence, of course, leaves a big gap. Since many children start to have problems when their parents divorce, if you are going it alone, you have a double burden at a time when you are usually depleted.

If your children are not with you, you may feel devastated by their loss. Though this happens to the father in the majority of cases, more and more women are experiencing this as increased numbers of men fight for and win custody rights. In either case, having to be a part-time parent can be extremely painful.

IMMEDIATE AFTERMATH PHASE

From the Children's Perspective

Brian, a bright, articulate 16-year-old, is frank about the difficulties of this phase:

> We used to be like the ideal American family, and now it's like a soap opera. My parents' relationship has actually gotten worse since they've split. They're both dating other people and they're both so jealous that all they do is fight about it. They try to get me to spy on each other, but I just play dumb. I miss my dad, but every time I go to see him, this stupid woman is there. So I just don't bother anymore. My mom is out so much with her new boyfriend and her new job, that I have to take care of my two brothers all the time or they'd be all alone. I've quit the football team and hardly see my friends. I'm too disgusted to care about even trying in school these days.

A major difficulty with this period for young people is that it takes their attention away from normal developmental issues that they should be working through for their age. Instead of focusing on schoolwork, peer relationships, the testing of independence, emerging values, and new identities, they are preoccupied with the many changes that have taken place in their home life.

Instead of having you and your spouse as two parents, they have one. If their custodial parent isn't adjusting well to the divorce, they often take on the burdensome and inappropriate role of friend or confidant. If that parent is also depressed or otherwise unhappy, a teen or young adult will often experience these same feelings themselves.

Children as Go-Betweens

This is the time when some parents slip into the unhealthy practice of using their children as go-betweens.

Instead of talking to each other directly about visitation or child support payments, they send messages through their teen or young adult. This places the young person in an extremely awkward position. They usually feel torn and conflicted, and often end up being depressed and confused as a result.

Absent Parent Grieved for Years

The parent who moves out, which is usually the father, is also often grieved for years. Even if those individuals were disappointing in reality, they tend to be idealized and deeply mourned when absent. Even if they visit regularly or have joint custody, the relationship has changed inalterably, and most children experience the loss of the relationship as they knew it before.

Your New Partner Felt as a Threat

Often your children will harbor the wish that you and your spouse will reunite. They will have active fantasies about that possibility. This naturally complicates things when you get involved with someone new. That person is inevitably seen as a threat who causes much anxiety for your children by their mere presence.

If one or both parents are dating or even married to someone else, your children can be overwhelmed by conflicting feelings. If they like the new person, they might feel disloyal to their parent. If they don't get along with the new person, it just makes them yearn even more for the days before the divorce. In many cases they feel deep discomfort at just having a stranger invade the privacy of their home life.

Fears of Abandonment

Young people commonly are jealous when either parent begins a new relationship because it threatens the special closeness that they share with that parent. In a real sense, they fear being abandoned again as they observe your affection and attention being directed to someone new.

Embarrassment at New Status

Young people must also live with the shame and embarrassment of being from a broken home. As common as divorce is today, most teens and young adults feel stigmatized and somehow abnormal when it happens to them.

If they start having serious problems themselves, they are of course doubly traumatized as a result. Drug or alcohol dependence, trouble in school or with the law, depression or any difficulties I mentioned earlier, seriously undermine a young person's self-esteem and prospects for normal development.

Outside Counseling Still Beneficial

If you have not received counseling earlier for yourself or your children, there is much to gain from doing it during this period. All the issues that have not been addressed can still be profitably worked on. If you have had counseling at earlier phases and you hit new snags as time goes by, it's worthwhile to take an objective look at things again. This is particularly true if conflict between you and your spouse continues, or if any of your teens or young adults are exhibiting signs of serious maladjustment.

THE LONG-RANGE PHASE

From the Parents' Perspective

Marcia, a 35-year-old housewife, isn't happy with her life since her divorce:

> Don't get me wrong, I've got a lot to be thankful for. Tom does give me the money I need, and that's important. But I still hate him for leaving me. And I don't want my kids going over there with that woman around. I know she tries to set them against me, just

by being so sweet and wonderful. She and my husband both spoil them rotten, and I'm afraid he's going to try some funny stuff with getting them back. That's why I try to limit the visits as much as possible. I'm seeing a man who's real nice and everything, but I don't know if I will ever want to marry him or anyone else for that matter. I just want things to be the way they used to be.

This is the time when things should have finally settled down. You and your former partner should be adjusted in your new lives. Ideally you should have worked out your mutual arrangements with children and finances so that there is little stress and conflict.

Of course, reality is often far from the ideal. As with the previous phase, either you or your partner might still be having difficulty as a divorced person. You might still feel lonely, depressed, and financially strapped. If one of you has successfully remarried and the other has not, this can cause deep-seated bitterness that still infects the relationship and both of your lives.

If one person has been unable to let go of the marriage, he or she might show hurt and anger by being uncooperative in making any arrangements that affect the children. Custody agreements and support payments are typical battlegrounds for smoldering feelings. Continued conflict during this late stage puts your children at considerable risk for developing a variety of behavioral and emotional disorders.

Even if you are both happily resettled into new lives, you have to continue to deal with your former spouse. The awkwardness of planning holidays, vacations, child visitation, and so on, constantly reminds you of your failed marriage.

If your children are having problems, you might feel remorse and guilt about their situation. Or you might feel anger that they are preventing you from finding happiness in your new life.

LONG-TERM PHASE

From the Children's Perspective

Eighteen-year-old Rebecca still feels she's suffering from her parent's divorce:

> It happened so long ago, you'd think I'd be over it. But I was so weirded out for so many years, that it really kind of changed me. I had been a good student before, but for most of high school when things were really tough, my grades were lousy. It's been real hard making up for that. I'm in junior college now, but I know I should be doing better than that. I just hate having to tell every new person I meet that my parents are divorced. It makes you feel like a marked person. I guess you might say I'm still depressed about the whole thing.

Many children are fairly well-adjusted to their parents' divorce by this stage. Earlier problems with school, depression, peers, and so on often disappear as they come to accept their new lives. Particularly if their custodial parent is relatively happy and the divorce has been somewhat amicable, teens and young adults can show considerable resiliency. Some even show greater maturity and self-reliance as the result of the divorce and the demands it made on them to help out at home and to work out important issues at an early age.

However, the opposite can also be true. If unhealthy patterns that began early in the divorce process were never adequately curbed, teens and young adults can be experiencing full-blown psychological and emotional adjustment disorders at this time. Ongoing battles between parents and the discomfort of dealing with new stepparents and siblings leaves many young people sad and dysfunctional. They can be confused in their own intimate relationships, which tend to be unsuccessful and unfulfilling for them. If they are experiencing serious clinical illnesses, such as chemical dependency or depression, their lives can seem like living nightmares.

Again, even if no help was sought earlier and your children are now in trouble, it is not too late to get them help. In my private practice and at The Regent Hospital, most of the young people I see fall into this category. Many have had serious problems for years. But they are young enough and flexible enough so that therapy can still make a dramatic difference for them. I have seen many young lives turned around in a matter of months, which is one of the great rewards of my work. Your involvement and concern is one of the biggest factors in getting your children back on the road to happy and productive lives.

Chapter 3

Understanding Your Children

In his pioneering book, *The Hurried Child,* David Elkind warned about the increasing tendency these days for parents to treat children as though they were "miniature adults." I have observed this also and as a result feel that it is important for you to understand that compared to adults, children are unformed and still developing emotionally and intellectually. Even teens and young adults, who in many ways seem well on their way to maturity, have not totally arrived.

Such things as dramatic growth spurts or an air of sophistication contribute to making young people *seem* mature, when in fact they still have many psychological and emotional stages to go through. Because of this, parents place expectations on their teens and young adults that are inappropriate for their age. When in the throes of divorce, this tendency becomes even more pronounced and can have particularly deleterious results because of the stress children are already experiencing due to the breakdown of the marriage.

In this chapter, I will review the different developmental stages of teens and young adults, along with the tasks that must be completed during each stage for full maturity to be attained. I will also discuss some special characteristics of adolescents and young adults that you should be aware of, point out some of the counterproductive things you might be doing, and offer some positive alternatives.

My goal is to give you a better understanding of what your children are going through, why they may be acting in certain ways and how the divorce process affects them. Ultimately I hope to help you find ways of dealing with them that will be beneficial to your whole family.

ADOLESCENCE A TIME OF RAPID CHANGE

When your children were infants you probably marveled at how quickly they changed. You greeted their first steps and first words with approval and encouragement. You viewed your toddler's early attempts at independence, such as a temper tantrum or an emphatic "no," as healthy expressions of natural development.

Because you realized that your infants and toddlers needed to develop their large muscles, you encouraged them to climb and run and ride tricycles. To help develop their fine motor skills, you probably bought them blocks and puzzles.

Adolescence Similar to First Two Years of Life

Early adolescence, which begins around age 10 or 11, compares to the first two years of life in the rapidity and number of changes the human organism experiences. Physical growth—which is easy to see—can come in sudden, dramatic spurts. And there are just as dramatic, though less tangible changes going on socially, emotionally, and intellectually as well.

Drastic Physical Changes

In early adolescence, physical appearance can undergo a rapid transformation. Arms and legs can become gangly and awkward, noses can get suddenly larger. Boys sometimes double their muscle mass between the ages of 12 and 16.

As hormones begin to surge, emerging sexual characteristics and urges throw a young person's whole sense of self off-balance. Changing voices in boys or the development of breasts in girls, along with the appearance of pubic hair, often cause real discomfort and embarrassment.

Children this age are understandably self-conscious and insecure. They worry about being popular and doing the right things. Their feelings are easily hurt and their self-esteem is fragile.

A Slow Process That Encompasses the Entire Being

The teens are a time when children's reasoning ability becomes refined, and they start the long process of sorting out values. Adjusting to a maturing body and mind is gradual and not complete until they reach their early twenties. During most of this time, young people are in a state of flux that leaves them self-absorbed and vulnerable.

Young Adults Still Growing, Too

Young people between 18 and 21 are often doing many adult things. They might have a full-time job and be paying you room and board if they are living at home. Or they might be away at college or a technical school, living independently, making many of their own decisions. Or they could be in the armed forces or even totally supporting themselves and living in their own apartment.

Young people this age are usually involved in some kind of serious relationship where they are learning how to be intimate and make commitments. They are also engaged in the serious business of testing their own competence and trying to find their place in the world.

All of these things are necessary for the completion of the task of achieving total independence from you. But the important thing to remember is that young people don't fully complete this task until they are at least 21 and in many cases 24 or 25. Consequently, they still need to feel that you are there, backing them up, emotionally and often financially as well.

Parents Might Not Be Sympathetic

If you are like most parents, you are aware of the difficulties of adolescence and young adulthood, but tend to be less sympathetic with your offspring at this time than when they were toddlers. Instead of encouraging their growth, you might actually do things that hamper it.

I will go into some of the common pitfalls you might encounter in dealing with young people this age later in this chapter. For now, I want to review the different developmental tasks that they must accomplish to further increase your understanding of the complexity of this period for your teens or young adults.

DEVELOPMENTAL TASKS OF ADOLESCENTS

Like infants and toddlers, adolescents have very specific developmental tasks that they must accomplish before they can proceed to the next stage, which for them is adulthood. If they are thwarted and don't accomplish these tasks, they simply won't mature as they should. If their environment is in turmoil, as it tends to be during a divorce, each task becomes more difficult.

Thrust Toward Independence

For example, the very thrust toward independence from you, which is the motivating force behind this entire period, can be derailed during the divorce process. As I noted earlier, if one parent is depressed or abusing alcohol or drugs and regularly turns to his or her children for emotional support, they may feel compelled to put aside their own needs to take care of the needs of that parent. They may go so far as to withdraw from friends and outside activities, forgoing vital opportunities to develop social skills and relationships as a result. If this goes on for too long, they can remain attached to that parent to an unhealthy degree for years. They might also get a false sense of their own maturity and make important judgment errors at a time when they should still be getting guidance from adults.

Identity Development

Another key task for young people this age is that of developing a coherent sense of who they are and who they will become as adults. Psychologist Erik Erikson described it as moving from a state of identity diffusion to identity integration. To do this properly, young people need the opportunity to experiment. Trying different hairstyles and clothes, changing their minds about what they want to be when they grow up, and falling in and out of love several times a year are all normal manifestations of this developmental stage in young people. Again, the volatile environment of a divorce is far from the ideal one for this kind of experimentation to take place. Instead of achieving a healthy and flexible sense of themselves, young people from divorced families often take on rigid identities that are prone to crack under stress.

Sexual and Aggressive Impulses

Another important developmental task for teens and young adults is that of mastery over surging sexual and aggressive drives. Here again, the atmosphere that tends to predominate during divorce is not conducive to helping young people in this task. Just when they should be learning how to negotiate conflicts in rational, socially acceptable ways, they are often experiencing open warfare at home on a regular basis. Just when they are wrestling with their own sexual impulses, they might have to grapple with the overwhelming fact of one of their parents having an affair with another person.

Intimacy and Commitment

Young people at this age are also working hard to learn the intricacies of intimacy and commitment. While some get involved in intense steady relationships early on, others have serial relationships throughout their teens as they flounder about in the tumultuous emotional waters of love and sex. At a time when they could really use good role models, their parents are demonstrating just how hard intimacy and commitment are to maintain.

Emerging Values

Teens and young adults are also involved in the important task of developing their own value system. When they were younger, things were more or less black and white. But as their reasoning capacity matures, they start to deal with the many ambiguities that life presents. They need time to ponder the gray areas and figure things out. They need those quiet moments to sit around with you and discuss whatever weighty issues are on their minds. If your marriage is breaking down and you and your spouse are going your separate ways, they don't have much of a forum for this process to occur. To fill the void, many children of divorce turn exclusively to peers for their values. Sometimes they literally grow up on the streets, which as we know all too well, can have disastrous results.

Acting Out

One of the delightful things about young people is how open and honest they tend to be about their feelings. We see this in how easily they can say "I hate you," or break down in tears when things don't go their way. This can be deceiving, however, because at the same time they are less likely to understand what's really bothering them. If something is especially painful, like the breakdown of your marriage, they may not even let their fears about this into their conscious minds, but instead will act out their feelings in any variety of negative ways. We call this behavioral defense against painful feelings "acting out."

It's helpful for you to be aware of this mechanism when trying to understand what is going on with your children. Just as you shouldn't unduly blame yourself for a failed marriage, you shouldn't blame your teens or young adults when their behavior deteriorates during your divorce. Your failing marriage is even more stressful for them than it is for you. Their negative behavior is only a reflection of their great unhappiness and confusion. I will go into detail about the different forms acting out can take in Chapter 6.

Divorce Very Difficult for Young People

As you can see, adolescence and young adulthood are enormously complex periods of growth and development. They are the last, but still very important stages of childhood. Because young people are experiencing so many changes themselves, a stable, predictable environment is the ideal one in which they can flourish.

As we have seen, and you probably have experienced yourself, a family in the midst of a divorce is far from this ideal. As I have indicated, the upheaval and confusion that it brings makes each developmental task all the more difficult to accomplish. Because you are in your own state of confusion, you are prone to making mistakes in dealing with your teens and young adults during a divorce. I will offer some constructive suggestions on ways to respond that should bring you better results.

COMMON PITFALLS

Being Unsympathetic

As I noted earlier, you were probably understanding of your children's displays of independence when they were toddlers. But when they show similar signs of pulling away from you as adolescents, you might not be as sympathetic.

Your response to oppositional behavior, such as backtalk, is a case in point. Instead of viewing it as a natural move toward independence, you may perceive it as a threat to your authority, and a simple heated discussion can disintegrate into an out-and-out battle. Instead of responding firmly but with underlying understanding, you may become very enraged and become overly restrictive or withdraw your support from your teen or young adult. Both responses create added tension for your adolescent and can alienate them from you. This can set up a negative pattern in which they shun all your guidance and advice at a time when they still need to learn many important things from you.

If your marriage is coming undone, this whole situation becomes exacerbated even further. You may be so overwhelmed by your divorce that your teen's or young adult's normal strivings toward independence become issues for conflict. Instead of being viewed as minor, natural deviances, their defiance can be blown way out of proportion and viewed as a major crime, which only leaves them feeling bad about themselves and out of sympathy with you.

Assuming Too Much Maturity

Parents often assume that their children can handle much more than is true for their age. This is especially common during the divorce process as you become preoccupied with yourself. Without even being aware of it, you might confide in your teen or young adult information about your sex life or your spouse's infidelities that is just too advanced for young minds and emotions to handle. Or you might turn to them for comfort and reassurance about your own fears and insecurities. Though this may seem natural if you have a close relationship and they seem eager to be of help, it is inappropriate.

Your children's needs for protection and for confidence in you are very strong. That doesn't mean you can't lean on them or expose your feet of clay once in a while. But if reversing roles becomes habitual, you are placing a great burden on them that can have negative consequences for years to come.

Abdicating Parental Responsibility

Or you might fall into the trap of thinking that your teens or young adults don't need as much attention and support as they did when they were younger. This is simply not true. Young people this age are going through so many changes and are vulnerable in so many ways, that your concern and involvement in their lives are of utmost importance to them. Unfortunately when the demands of a divorce start to take over, I have seen all too many parents abdicate their responsibilities and more or less let their teens or young adults raise themselves.

Scapegoating

We all know the term scapegoating as it applies in society. But it is a phenomenon that can occur in families as well and is one that you should be aware of when trying to understand yourself and your children.

Essentially, in society at large and in families, scapegoating is a psychological mechanism that people use to avoid facing negative things about themselves. Though we all have undesirable traits, we have a strong need to see ourselves in a positive light. Admitting our faults causes us anxiety and discomfort. Consequently, we tend to repress these negative views of ourselves and project them out onto others. In society, whole groups become the convenient target or scapegoat for attributes we do not wish to see in ourselves.

This mechanism can also occur in families, particularly when there is dysfunction, as is true in a bad marriage or during a divorce. For example, in the early dissolution phase, you and your spouse might be arguing frequently. But because it is too anxiety-producing, you might not have admitted yet that your marriage is really in trouble. Sensing the tension and confusion, one of your children might start seriously misbehaving or acting out, as was explained previously. Rather than admit to yourself the painful reasons for your failing marriage, you project your negative feelings onto your child, who then becomes the target for all that is wrong with the family. Hyperactive, "difficult" children or those with learning disabilities are often the victims of this kind of scapegoating.

Or you might project all the bad traits that you see in your spouse onto your child—"you're just like your father or your mother" is an expression with unpleasant connotations that we've all heard too often. Sometimes if parents are afraid to be directly angry or critical of the spouse, they will take that aggression out on the scapegoated child. Tragically, the child often accepts the role of being the "no-good" one or the "black sheep," and gets on a path of self-defeating behavior that can continue for life.

Sometimes it seems as though the child willingly takes on the role of the "bad one" or the "sick one," because the young person realizes that it keeps the parents from dealing directly with the possible breakup of the marriage. Sometimes caring for a sick or deviant child is the only thing that couples can do well together. And focusing on this "problem" can divert their attention for years from facing their own.

Spouses can also scapegoat each other, with one having to believe that the other is the "bad guy" and totally at fault for the marriage's failure. This prevents the individual from having to admit faults, and has the unfortunate consequence of prolonging bitterness and blame while postponing healing.

These are just a few examples of the many forms scapegoating can take. It is a complex phenomenon, and I point it out to you just so you can be attuned to the possibility of it occurring in your own family. If you suspect that you might be scapegoating one of your children or your spouse, or that you might be the victim of it yourself, you might want to consider talking this over with a professional counselor for advice on how to rectify the situation.

Special Problems of Young Adults

If you are going through a divorce, all of the normal issues that young adults must grapple with become more complicated. If you are still supporting them financially, this can be a tricky point to negotiate even under the best of circumstances. They may be doing things that you don't approve of, yet their age makes it hard to interfere. If you are footing the bills, you may still feel entitled to have some control over their behavior. Disagreement between you and your spouse, or by now your ex, over who pays what for your young adult, just adds another issue to an already crowded agenda.

If you are in the phase of starting a new family, your young adult has to deal with all the complexities that this presents in addition to her or his own problems. If things don't work out for them, either in new relationships, at school, or in the work world, they sometimes need a safe haven where they can retreat temporarily and regroup before moving on. If they are uncomfortable with you and your new spouse or stepchildren for any reason, this can rob them of such a place. This in turn can make them feel that they are being thrust into adulthood prematurely, and some react with panic and rage. The result may be that they thrash around on their own and behave impulsively, sometimes getting into deeper problems that otherwise could have been averted.

According to researcher Barbara S. Cain, young adults can experience "a temporary moral derailment" during a divorce. This occurs because their parents' behavior—be it infidelity, sexual promiscuity, or the breaking of the marriage commitment itself—seems a direct contradiction to all they had taught their children as being right and respectable. Young people this age are often left feeling "disillusioned, disoriented, and morally adrift." Having lost their parents as moral exemplars, youngsters' reactions range from "defiant self-indulgence to abstemious pleasure avoidant behavior."

WHAT YOU CAN DO

Being There for Your Kids

During a crisis such as a divorce, you should go out of your way to be sensitive to your teens or young adults. Set aside special time to be with them, either just to have fun together or to talk about their concerns. Let them know that you understand how difficult your divorce is for them. Give them the opportunity to ask you questions and discuss whatever is on their minds. Being there for children, emotionally and physically, can be very constructive.

If you are having some of the problems with your

young adult that I mentioned above, being sensitive to him or her is the first step toward a successful resolution. You and your ex-spouse should try to resolve your differences over finances without involving your child. If this seems impossible, counseling is advised.

It's also important to let your young adult know that you are still there for them and that there is a place to come home to when life gets too tough. If you do have a new family, this might take a heroic effort on your part, but could make a crucial difference in your child's life.

Discipline with Love Especially Important

It is also important that you continue to set realistic and age-appropriate limits on your teens' or young adults' behavior during this time and stay in a routine as much as possible. Divorce brings with it an inevitable sense of chaos, which these last two measures tend to counterbalance. Many experts feel that being firm and consistent, but at the same time very affectionate, with children yields the best results under any circumstances. During a divorce I would say that this is a particularly worthwhile approach.

Research has shown, and I have found it to be true in my own experience, that the quality of the parent-child relationship can offset the negative aspects—even parental conflict—of divorce.

Understanding Essential

As I noted earlier, young people need to experiment with different identities as part of their natural development.

Sympathy and patience on your part are vital in helping them achieve a sense of themselves that is not overly rigid. This is necessary so that they can withstand stress and end up with a healthy sense of themselves.

You also have to achieve a delicate balance between support, limit setting, and allowing them freedom. There are no magic formulas for this. But it does require that you think about what you are doing and be flexible enough to change your behavior if you are not getting good results. If you find this hard to do on your own, getting professional guidance may be the answer.

Openness Important

Protecting your children from the wrong kind of information does not mean that you should hide things from them. Being open and honest about the important details of your divorce is essential for their well-being. Telling them age-appropriate facts, such as "Daddy and I aren't able to work out our differences, so we are getting a divorce. But we still love you. And we will always be your parents," helps them to understand what is going on without overloading them. Also filling them in on dates and times of events—when one parent will be moving out, when and if you will change your residence—lets them know what to expect, which is vital for all of us during a crisis.

Keeping Open Conflict to a Minimum

Because young people this age are learning the important task of mastering their aggressive impulses, controlling your own during a divorce is of utmost importance. Seeing you and your spouse constantly battling and perhaps even engaging in violent behavior is extremely damaging to children and sends them all the wrong messages. Therefore it is crucial that you avoid serious battling in front of them at all costs. If this seems impossible, you really should get marital counseling to help you resolve your differences in a nonhostile manner.

Dealing with Issues of Sexuality and Commitment

In a healthy marriage, sexual relations between parents are discreet. Affection is expressed, but overt sexual discussions are not carried on in front of children. During a divorce, sexual issues, particularly infidelity, may come out in open conflict. Or when one parent is dating, children may be forced to consider that the sexual needs of the parents are being indulged. These situations can be very upsetting at a time when youngsters are grappling with their own confusing sexual urges.

Essentially, the best way to handle all matters of sexuality is to try to be as discreet and sensitive as possible. Avoid discussing your sexual problems. If infidelity is an issue, try to underplay the sexual aspects of it if your child becomes aware that you or your spouse is involved with another person. If you are dating, keep open displays of affection to a minimum and avoid completely any overtly sexual behavior in front of your children. Don't have your lover stay overnight if at all possible.

In general, my advice would be to even avoid bringing a new person home at all until you are sure the relationship is serious. It overburdens young people emotionally if different people keep appearing and disappearing as potential new stepparents. It also further confuses their already confused sense of the meaning of commitment in a relationship.

Take Care of Yourself

If you are feeling overwhelmed about any aspect of your divorce, you should try to get yourself some help. As I stressed earlier, divorce is a major trauma for most people and there's no reason to assume that you should be superhuman and handle it all by yourself. Individual counseling can do you a world of good at this time.

Relieving pressure on yourself goes a long way to helping you to be a better parent. Talking to another adult enables you to avoid the pitfall of leaning too much on your teens or young adults. It can also free up your mind so that you can devote more time to thinking about and paying attention to your children.

If you can't afford individual therapy, there might be a support group for divorcees in your area that you could attend. This kind of self-help program can be very beneficial; I will discuss it further in a later chapter.

Chapter 4

Parental Warfare: Roots and Remedies

Lily, a quiet, sad 18-year-old, talks about her parents' fighting.

> My parents fought all the time. They got so angry that it sounded like they hated each other... like they were going to kill each other. My brothers and I would get so scared that we'd lock ourselves in my room and sit on the bed in a huddle, all hugging each other till it stopped. To this day, when I see my father getting angry, I freeze up. I cry if my boyfriend even looks at me cross-eyed. He says I'm being too sensitive, and that it makes him angry that I'm so touchy. But I can't help it.

Trying to understand her parents' relationship still causes great anguish for Susan, a thoughtful, serious 25-year-old.

> It's never been really out in the open what was wrong between them, and that's what's made it so hard. They have always acted pleasant enough on the surface, but there was always this tension and snide

comments behind each other's backs. And it's still that way today. They've been divorced for over 10 years, but they still dig at each other all the time. It just hurts so much for me because I love them both and I want things to be nice and happy like in other people's families. But it never is. It's all bitterness and nastiness. And I'm caught in the middle.

Sixteen-year-old Tom, speaks with a trembling voice when he recalls the violence in his home.

Watching him hit my mom like that used to make me crazy. I felt so helpless. I wanted to kill him, and I still hate him for it. The worst part is that now my stepfather does the same thing and she puts up with it. I let him have it whenever I can, but I hate fighting. I hate the whole thing. I just wish my mother could get away from it all and get herself some help. Find herself a nice guy for a change.

I know it's affected me. The other day I actually smacked my girlfriend in the face, and I felt terrible afterward. I don't know if she'll ever forgive me and it scares me. I'm afraid someday I might really hurt somebody.

WHAT WENT WRONG?

Remember your wedding day? You were probably excited, nervous, full of hope and anticipation. You probably felt very much in love with your future mate. Even if you had some lingering doubts, chances are you were sincerely expecting to spend the rest of your life with the person with whom you walked down the aisle, or stood in front of the judge or the justice of the peace to exchange those ancient vows.

Looking back, you may wonder how all that love and hope turned to so much anger and disappointment. You probably ask yourself how that person who was supposed to bring you happiness has instead caused you such pain. How did those early words of love turn into recriminations and put-downs?

By the same token, when you first had children, you probably did everything possible to protect and comfort them. You wrapped them in the softest blankets, tiptoed around when they were sleeping, buttoned them up in the warmest clothes before taking them out in the cold, and soothed their tears with lullabies and hugs.

How is it then, you might wonder, when things started to go wrong between you and your spouse, that you didn't take those same precautions to protect them from pain and fear? Unfortunately, when in the throes of passion, all too many parents forget that their children are just as vulnerable, if not even more so, to destructive warfare between them as they are to any stresses in the environment.

As a result, children are exposed to hateful scenes that cause them great emotional pain and do long-lasting damage.

THE PARADOX OF LOVE AND MARRIAGE

There is a paradox of love and marriage that helps to explain why our early good intentions so often go awry. The very intensity of the positive feelings that you have for your mate is what makes those feelings so easily transform into their opposites. Because you have so much deep emotion invested in that important other, when things start to go sour, love can quickly turn to anger.

HEALTHY VS. UNHEALTHY ANGER

Anger is a normal, healthy emotion and should be expressed in a forthright manner so that it can lead to resolution of conflicts. It is my experience that many people are confused about anger and that their mismanagement of it leads to much destructiveness in relationships. Rather than expressing it openly, they try to repress it. Or they bring old anger that they have been harboring from other situations into their relationship. As a result, anger often becomes perverted and comes out in all kinds of destructive ways.

Over time, perverted anger between people often leads to feelings of hatred or even to violence. Perverted anger can set off a chain of negative feelings that often feed on and perpetuate themselves. Because it is so important to understand, I'm going to deal with the issue of anger in greater depth at different points throughout this chapter.

CHILDREN GET LOST IN THE COMMOTION

You should, of course, try to protect your children under all circumstances. But because they are part of your family and so intimately involved in your everyday affairs, you might in a sense forget that they are even there or are in hearing range when a fight erupts between you and your spouse. Because your negative emotions can be so intense, your normal feelings of protectiveness for your children can simply get drowned out in the commotion. But as you can see from the experiences described above, children are very much aware of what goes on between their parents and very vulnerable to its effects. If they witness violence or are objects of violence, this can be especially scarring.

Consequently, I am going to explore with you the common reasons behind marital anger and warfare, the many forms it can take, and the effects it has on children, and try to offer more positive ways you and your spouse can handle your differences both during and after a divorce. I'm going to focus in on substance abuse and depression as causes of divorce, because I believe they are more commonly at the root of marital problems than most people realize and as a result are often overlooked.

IDEALIZE POTENTIAL PARTNER

No matter how well you knew the person you intended to marry, you probably idealized him or her. You didn't notice your differences as much as the things that you had in common. This is what being in love is all about. But after the honeymoon was over, as the saying goes, and the reality of living with your spouse day to day set in, basic differences inevitably emerged that couldn't be ignored or denied. Perhaps you had different spending habits, or you disagreed on how to raise the children. Or maybe you became aware that your spouse drank much more than you had realized.

CONTROL ISSUES

Though these kinds of differences can be worked out if two people are truly committed to each other and want the marriage to work, very often they become issues of control where one person tries to change the other. If the person who is expected to change feels they are being coerced and resents this, a fierce power struggle often sets in that becomes the source of all kinds of disagreements and arguments. If these differences are never resolved, they often undo a marriage over time.

MARITAL ISSUES TEND TO BE EXPLOSIVE

The most common issues that tend to undermine a marriage are, as I have discussed previously, different spending and parenting styles, sexual incompatibility, and infidelity. They can be so detrimental to a marriage because they go to the very core of who we are as individuals and what we believe is right. Altering such basic things about ourselves is not easy and requires an underlying commitment by both partners that the marriage is worth saving above all else.

Chemical dependency and depression are hard on a marriage because of the profoundly negative effect they have on an individual's behavior. Both can contribute to parental warfare and can also be exacerbated in either or both partners by marital strife.

MISMANAGEMENT OF ANGER

Not knowing how to manage anger effectively is at the root of much parental warfare. Most of us are never taught that it is okay to be angry with the person we love and that it is all right to express this. Most of us don't realize that there are healthy and unhealthy ways to do this. As a result, people either hold anger in so that it comes out in indirect ways, or they attack each other head-on, which always worsens things.

I find that most of my patients are confused about anger, and I therefore spend a lot of time educating them on how to manage it effectively in their lives and in their important relationships. As part of this process, I give them all copies of *The Angry Book* by Theodore Isaac Rubin, M.D. I strongly recommend that you and your spouse both read this to help you understand this important emotion in all of its complexities. And at the end of this chapter I will offer some pointers on ways to manage your anger that should lead to more constructive resolution of your differences than warfare ever does.

HOW SUBSTANCE ABUSE UNDERMINES A MARRIAGE

As I noted earlier, chemical dependency is one of the leading psychiatric disorders of the decade. One of the hallmarks of chemical dependency is the tendency for those involved to employ the defense mechanism known as *denial*. Essentially, denial means what it says, the refusal to see or admit something to oneself even though it may be perfectly obvious.

People are always aware on some level—especially today with the subject so much in the public eye—that they are using a dangerous substance when they drink regularly or use drugs. But because they are developing a physical and psychological dependence on that substance for some kind of comfort, they often rationalize away its dangers and minimize the actual amount they are taking.

Any time denial is used, there is danger of the unpleasant thoughts or feelings that are repressed being projected out onto someone else who then becomes a scapegoat, as I explained in the previous chapter. In chemical dependency this tendency becomes even more pronounced because the taking of any drug often leaves a person irritable and weakens their normal constraints against expressing negative emotions. Consequently, the chemically dependent person often engages in blaming his or her partner or children for all that is wrong. It's not difficult to see how this can inflame a relationship and create an atmosphere where warfare flourishes. Also, if the other partner demands that the chemically dependent person change, the battle lines get drawn over issues of control, as I mentioned earlier, which further exacerbates things.

The damage that such behavior causes children can be extreme. Children who are victims of a blaming and irritable parent often have severely impaired self-esteem. As a result they may suffer a clinical depression and feel responsible for all that is wrong with their parents' marriage or all that is wrong with the world. Or they may go through life with diminished expectations, never fully realizing their potential for achievement. The unreliability and unpredictability of a chemically dependent parent can also impede the development of a young person's normal feelings of trust in others, which can hamper their ability to form intimate relationships.

THE IMPORTANCE OF DIAGNOSING SUBSTANCE ABUSE

As I noted in Chapter 1, chemical dependency usually affects a person's behavior in many ways that negatively impact on a marriage. The reckless spending habits, diminished parenting ability and sexual performance, and the tendency toward infidelity that go hand in hand with substance abuse cause much friction and outright battling between couples. But because of the tendency of one or both partners to deny that there is a drinking or drug abuse problem, these behaviors rather than the chemical dependency itself, are often seen as the reason for the breakup.

I point this out because I believe that if you recognize that substance abuse is the true cause of your differences, you can address the problem by seeking treatment and perhaps avert a divorce. I can't tell you how many of my patients have looked back on the shamble of their lives and sadly realized this too late.

By the same token, divorce or the threat of divorce can push vulnerable individuals further along the path of chemical dependency. If the problem continues after divorce, it can continue to negatively affect the entire family for years to come if it is not correctly diagnosed and treated.

Effects on Children

Since chemical dependency tends to run in families and is thought to have a biological basis, it is important to recognize it so proper preventive measures can be taken for your children as well. If untreated in one or both parents, children are even at greater risk for developing this condition because of the increased turmoil and tension it inevitably visits upon a family.

If Substance Abuse Untreated, Divorce May Be Only Solution

As I noted earlier, if chemically dependent people refuse to get help for their problem, divorce may be the only solution. Untreated chemical dependency is very harmful to a relationship and a family. There is no reason why anyone should suffer the consequences of someone else's unwillingness to get treatment for what is a very treatable disorder. In fact, staying in such a relationship often actually keeps the chemically dependent person from ever facing and having to deal with the seriousness of their addiction. Sometimes divorce or the threat of divorce can be the impetus for that individual to get help.

If you or your partner are using either drugs or alcohol and know or fear that a dependence is developing, my advice to you is to seek professional advice from someone qualified to treat this disorder. Diagnosing the problem and getting professional help is the most intelligent way to address this kind of problem. I will discuss treatment alternatives for substance abuse in Chapter 6.

DEPRESSION SIMILAR TO SUBSTANCE ABUSE

Depression, along with chemical dependency, is the other leading psychiatric disorder of our times. Left untreated, it can affect a family and undermine a marriage in many of the same ways that chemical dependency does.

Depressed people are essentially unavailable emotionally as a parent and a partner. If they are not getting treatment, chances are they are denying that they even have a problem. Though we tend to think of depressed people as being sad, listless and withdrawn, they can also be hostile, angry, and belligerent. As with the chemically dependent, depressed individuals can scapegoat and blame other family members. If there isn't outright warfare, the depressed parent at times casts a pall over the entire atmosphere of a household, which can infect other members as effectively as a virus.

Effects of Depressed Parent on Children

Children of depressed parents are often depressed themselves and feel responsible for that parent's unhappiness. Since mood disorders tend to run in families and are thought to have a biological basis just as chemical dependency does, children of depressed parents are at greater risk of developing this disorder than others.

If Depression Untreated, Divorce May Be Only Solution

As with chemical dependency, because it is so damaging to a relationship and a family, I would say that when individuals refuse to get help for depression, their partners may be left with no choice but to seek a divorce. Depression is a biologically based disorder which is treatable with proper medication and counseling. If you suspect that you or your partner may be suffering a clinical depression, seek professional advice from someone who is qualified to treat this disorder.

GROWING UP IN A BATTLE ZONE

Just how harmful is parental warfare for children? As you can see from the quotes in the beginning of this chapter, it often leaves deep emotional scars. Children can feel responsible for the fights and harbor deep guilt that they carry around for life. Or there are just the bad memories that haunt them, sometimes to the point of causing seriously neurotic behavior. One of my patients was so traumatized by her parents' habit of arguing at the dinner table, that she developed a full-blown eating disorder. She was so crippled by anxiety from her childhood memories of these battles that as a young adult she was physically unable to enjoy a meal at a restaurant with friends.

Emotional Resonance

Young people are really much closer to their emotions than we are. They haven't learned yet to hide them in themselves or deny seeing them in others. They are especially attuned to what we as their parents are feeling and sometimes know what is going on with us before we do ourselves. When there is rancor and battling between you and your spouse, the atmosphere of your home becomes contaminated. It is like throwing poison into a fish bowl and clouding the very medium in which the helpless captives must live.

Feelings of Insecurity

Children who grow up in a battle zone can have deep-seated feelings of insecurity and don't believe that the world is a safe place. It's very confusing if the two people who are supposed to protect them and are supposed to love each other are always fighting and putting each other down. Children also often develop rage toward the person who is doing the maligning. And this feeling sometimes translates into violent behavior on the young person's part without understanding its source. If children witness or directly experience violence, they are even more likely to repeat this in their own relationships, either as the victim, if they are female, or the perpetrator, if they are male.

Feel Torn

Using children as go-betweens or sniping about each other to your offspring engenders tremendous conflict in them. I have a 14-year-old boy on our unit at The Regent Hospital who was depressed to the point of being suicidal after years of being the victim of just such behavior. This was dramatized one day as he sat in my office between his parents and his head swiveled from side to side as though he were watching a tennis match as he turned to listen to each of them. Pointing this out to him and his parents and, most important, convincing his parents to change their behavior was a significant turning point in freeing this young man from his life-threatening depression.

Learn Destructive Problem-Solving Style

The family is the place where we all learn how to behave in the world. If fighting and arguing are the norm there, children assume that this is the way families act. They come to believe that adults solve things by overpowering each other. They never learn constructive ways to resolve differences and tend to repeat the destructive patterns of their parents in their own relationships.

Manipulative Behavior

Children who grow up in real war zones often develop conning behavior just to survive. Sometimes lying and being manipulative are the only ways to get food and shelter. Similarly, if parents are locked in ongoing battles, children must often resort to unhealthy means to get what they need.

An example is when young people try to get their way by complaining to one parent about the unfairness of the other when the latter attempts to set limits on them. If parents regularly fall for this and give in to unreasonable demands, manipulative behavior can become part of young persons' personalities. Consequently, they get labeled as "bad seeds" whom nobody trusts and few people like. It's important to remember that such manipulative behavior is not children's fault, but is merely an adaptive response: a way for them to get what they need from an unhealthy system.

During divorce, parents are often so preoccupied that they aren't providing their offspring adequate love and attention. When their children start lying and playing one parent off the other in attempts to get their needs fulfilled, they are viewed as bad instead of as desperate and confused. Often when I get to know young people like this, there is real sadness underneath their cool exteriors.

Don't Know Whom to Believe

Also, developing values and major life decisions might be forestalled if parents can't come to some agreement on important issues. For example, I had one very bright young woman as a patient who didn't finish college because her divorced parents had differing views on the importance of her doing so. Not to have gotten an education beyond high school could have been a real tragedy for her because she probably never would have achieved the level of success that she was innately capable of.

THE MANY FACES OF PARENTAL WARFARE

"We have arguments, but we never really fight" or "We have a very civilized relationship" are the kinds of comments I sometimes hear from people when discussing the issue of parental warfare. I rarely take what they say at face value.

This is because parental warfare often isn't out in the open and as a result parents might not even be aware that they are engaged in destructive battling. Consequently, I'm going to list the different forms it can take to help you evaluate your own behavior.

- Open conflict, name-calling.
- Physical violence.
- "Silent" battles in which anger is not openly but rather behaviorally expressed. This can take the forms of angry or disapproving looks, sighs, or emotional distancing between partners.
- Sniping, either directly to each other or in front of the children when one partner is absent.
- Trying to turn the children against the other spouse, either subtly or with direct tactics.
- Actually involving the children in battles.
- Using children as spies or go-betweens.
- Custody battles in which children are ripped apart.

KEEPING THE CAP ON PARENTAL WARFARE

Now that I've pointed out the damage that warfare between you and your partner can wreak on your children, you are at a point where you must make a decision. If you truly want to protect your children and minimize the hurt from your unsuccessful marriage and divorce, you have to decide to make that goal a priority over whatever bad feelings you have about your spouse.

Once you have made that decision, the power is in your hands to find ways to do whatever is possible to work out your disagreements in a more constructive fashion than has been your habit. Though this may seem like a monumental task at first, I can assure you that the positive effects that this can result in for your children are well worth the effort.

Indeed one study has shown that spouses' satisfaction with each other's parenting and support after divorce is correlated with a number of important positive behaviors in children, particularly for boys, including better school performance and fewer problems overall.

Reducing warfare between you and your spouse can have many positive benefits for you as well. If you are both going to be involved in continued parenting of your children, as I highly recommend, it will simply be much easier for you if your relationship is cooperative. Anger and hostility are a drain on your energy and keep you from the important task of rebuilding your life.

LETTING GO OF YOUR ANGER

There's nothing like a strong dose of righteous indignation to start your juices flowing and infuse your life with a glowing sense of self-justification. I'm being facetious about this and don't mean to trivialize the real hurt you might feel as a result of your divorce. But sometimes it seems that people actually use their anger almost as a tonic, if not even a drug. Not only do they seem to relish working themselves up into a pitch of emotion about all the wrongs their partner has committed, but many no doubt find refuge behind their anger as well. By putting all the blame on someone else, they never have to look at themselves or take any responsibility for the failed marriage.

As I stressed earlier, anger is a healthy emotion that needs direct expression and you should learn to manage it in a positive fashion. You might have very valid reasons for feeling much anger about what has gone on between you and your spouse. But no matter how justified you may feel in being angry, holding onto it for too long can be very self-destructive.

It is just plain stressful and bad for you to go around seething all of the time. If preoccupied with angry and hurtful feelings, you are less likely to move on with important things that could bring you satisfaction. It's hard to start a new relationship if you're in a bad mood all of the time. No one really wants to hear how wronged someone has been too many times; it gets boring after a while.

There is also really nothing to be gained from blaming your partner for all that has gone wrong with your marriage. It's important to remember what the things are that are driving you apart. If it's different styles of spending money or of parenting, or sexual incompatibility, these are things that are really no one's fault. Rather than blaming your partner, it's much more realistic and healthy for you to just accept that these are things neither of you can easily change.

If you really love each other and want the marriage to work, most differences can usually be surmounted, especially if counseling is sought. If you feel they can't be resolved, it does neither of you any good and actually does harm, to hang onto the notion that one person is wrong or bad just because they disagree with you even on important matters. For both of your sakes, for the children's sake, you should put bad feelings behind you as much as possible since getting along will make everyone's life dramatically easier.

ANGER OF SPOUSE OF THE CHEMICALLY DEPENDENT OR DEPRESSED

As I noted earlier, the chemical dependency and depression of one partner cause a special kind of frustration for spouses. Denial, blaming behavior of the affected person, and so forth, engender their own anger in partners which can be particularly hard to let go of. If someone refuses to get help it can lead to all kinds of feelings of disgust, resentment and even rage in the partner who feels victimized.

But even here, in the long run it is much more productive for the persons who are not ill to view their partners with compassion rather than anger. They are, after all, probably biologically predisposed to their condition. It is not something they consciously and willingly chose. And it is hard for many people to acknowledge that they need help.

MANAGING ANGER

Managing anger means putting it to use for the constructive resolution of our differences. To do that you should try to recognize its sources. Though these can be varied, generally you feel anger when frustrated, when threatened, offended, or inconvenienced. Since anger is just part of being alive, expressing it in a healthy manner is important for your health and that of your relationships. If you let it out at the time that you feel it, it should ideally just go away. If you hold it in, it's just going to build up and come out in indirect and usually more damaging ways.

Sarcastic remarks, subtle put-downs, or emotional distancing can all be the indirect expression of suppressed resentment. They tend to be more hurtful than a fair expression of anger, because they can set off a vicious cycle of hurtful behaviors that lead to more anger and so on.

OWNING ANGER

A key to managing anger is to own it. By that I mean not to blame the other person for it, but to recognize that it is something that comes from within you. Your anger may arise from deeply held values or just from your annoyance at being inconvenienced or not given your due in life. Or you may have a need to feel superior to your spouse and actually derive some hidden satisfaction from the anger that you feel for him or her. Though your partner's behavior may indeed seem outrageous and a justifiable reason for your anger, remember that not everyone would find that behavior objectionable. Even seemingly innocuous things like an individual's going to church can cause resentment in some people.

If you find yourself getting angry at your partner's spending habits, it is much more constructive to say, "I feel anxious when you spend money on expensive clothes." This leaves the door open for negotiation. You have put your partner in a position to feel some compassion for you. If instead, you go on the attack, the results will be quite different. A statement such as "The way you spend money is so irresponsible it makes me furious," is very likely to put the other person on the defensive. Such an attacking and blaming approach causes more resentment and rarely get anyone to change his or her behavior. Even if the behavior is much more offensive, such as substance abuse or infidelity, you are much more likely to come to some kind of understanding with your partner if you own your anger and don't go on the offense.

Resentment Lists

One of the ways I try to help my patients manage it is to have them compose resentment lists about important people in their lives. Many will say, "Oh, I can't feel angry at my mother. She is so wonderful to me." Somehow they feel they can't be angry with someone they love. But this is not true. We all inevitably do things that rub each other the wrong way. Not to acknowledge this and talk about these things, as I noted above, leads to lots of covert behaviors that usually do more to undermine a relationship than the healthy expression of anger ever does.

Sense of Humor Important

I also always urge my patients to try to look at things with a sense of humor. It's amazing what a salve laughter can be for healing all kinds of hurts.

RULES OF FAIR PARENTAL WARFARE

- Avoid those subjects that you know you can't ever seem to agree on. If it is vital that they be worked out, do so with a counselor if all else fails.
- Couch statements carefully. Avoid blaming and attacking your partner. Instead of saying, "You make me angry," try saying "I feel upset (or angry, or hurt or scared, etc.) when you do thus and so."
- Have your family make resentment lists about each other. Then sit down and discuss them, with everyone having a chance to air their beefs in a non-attacking manner. Use it as a time to negotiate change with each other.
- Try to cultivate a sense of humor about your differences whenever possible. After the divorce, some people find the development of a teasing, bantering relationship free of barbs and resentment goes a long way to defusing tension.
- After the divorce, if you and your spouse just can't be civil, try to meet on neutral ground or in a public place where you are more likely to feel constrained.
- If you can't avoid destructive battling when you are together, at least avoid fighting in front of the children.
- Never use your children as go-betweens, spies or messengers.
- Never involve your children in fights.
- Don't put your partner down in front of your children.
- Where financial issues are concerned, try to be as businesslike as possible. Don't get your children caught in the middle.
- Do not stand for or engage in violent behavior of any kind. If this becomes a part of your relationship which you can't control, seek professional help immediately.
- If either you or your spouse seem to be "angry" individuals—harboring bad feelings, unable to deal with anger constructively—seek professional help.

Chapter 5

The Double Whammy of a Failed Marriage and Floundering Kids

Marty, a successful 38-year-old insurance salesman, feels overwhelmed about what is going on in his life:

> I did everything I could to save the marriage, but Susan would have none of it. She just couldn't forgive me for having that affair. My kids have really fallen apart since I moved out, and I blame myself for the whole thing. Denise is running around with a rough bunch, and I'm sure she's having sex with that creepy guy she's been dating. Nick's grades have fallen and he seems so angry and belligerent all of the time that I barely recognize him. I'm just hoping that they'll eventually adjust and forgive me someday.

Marcia, a 40-year-old bank executive and mother of two teenaged boys, expresses true bewilderment at her sons' growing problems:

> I thought the divorce was going to improve things for all of us. My husband and I weren't getting along for so many years and I was tired of his drinking. A new life with a new man seemed the only solution.

> When I met Al, he seemed perfect, so I went for it. Now five years later, my life is a nightmare. Both my sons are drinking heavily and doing drugs. Both have gotten into trouble with the law. My ex-husband just moved away, and Al and I are overwhelmed with handling them. He's tried to be understanding, but I think he's beginning to wonder what he himself got into.

Angelo, a 45-year-old policeman, is just beginning to make sense of all that has gone wrong in recent years in his life:

> When my wife, Natalie, started to change several years ago, I chalked it up to the fact that we had just moved and she needed time to adjust. But she got worse and worse to the point that she sat around all day and moped. She always said she felt depressed, but I thought that it was only a female thing. When I finally realized that she needed help it was too late. My daughter Cathy and I both were very depressed just living with her. I met another woman at work and we got involved. When I told Natalie I wanted a divorce, it was like she didn't care. But Cathy really came undone. Her grades dropped and she just withdrew from the world entirely. But it wasn't till she took that overdose of sleeping pills that I realized she was really in trouble and needed professional help.

EVERYONE IS GOING TO HAVE SOME REACTION.

Divorce *can* be a solution, sometimes it's the *only* solution to an impossibly bad marriage. But people are often unprepared for just how hard it is on their children. Often they are overwhelmed when their sons and daughters start acting in ways and doing things that seem totally out of character or run the risk of getting them into serious trouble.

Not all children react badly to divorce. And for some of those that do, their problems can be transitory, fading with the passage of time and perhaps even in some ways strengthening their character in the long run. But for a significant portion of young people, the trauma of their parents' divorce sets into motion adverse reactions that turn into crises in themselves.

DETERMINING IF IT'S SERIOUS OR NOT?

We all know that adolescence can be a tough time. If you didn't realize it before, I hope that what you have read here so far has made you aware that a divorce can heap its own special difficulties on young people this age. Most teens and young adults are going to show some symptoms of their anger, displeasure, confusion, and emotional upset at the breakup of their parents' marriage.

But telling the difference between "normal" reactions to divorce and serious ones is crucial. I can't tell you how many parents come to me after years of acting out or depressive behavior on the part of their children and say, "Oh, I just thought it was typical teenage stuff. I didn't want to overreact." All too often their teen or young adult has progressed far into the stages of a chemical dependency, mood disorder or the likes that could have been averted or greatly ameliorated if the proper treatment had been obtained earlier.

Therefore it is my purpose in this chapter to alert you to the specific reactions that can be triggered by a divorce and to offer guidelines to help you evaluate whether or not they are truly serious.

BIOPSYCHOSOCIAL DISEASE MODEL

In helping my patients and when teaching psychiatry students in medical school, I use a disease model to explain the different forces that contribute to an individual's breakdown. As you can see, basically three factors are involved:

Biological predisposition. Today it is recognized that individuals are born with certain vulnerabilities or predispositions for disease that they have inherited from their parents. These include vulnerabilities for physical disorders, such as diabetes and heart disease, as well as those for psychological ones. For our purposes here we are only interested in those in the psychological realm, such as chemical dependency, depression, or any form of mental illness.

Stressors. Life is full of stresses, which can trigger breakdowns in individuals with biological predispositions. Life's big stresses include death, illness, poverty, natural disasters, accidents, financial problems, and, as you realize by now, divorce.

Enabling System. This is a combination of factors in individuals' environment which enable illnesses to progress unchecked. Enabling systems usually involve denial or some sort of misunderstanding by significant others about what is really wrong so that individuals do not get the treatment they need.

Because we believe that these three factors all contribute to the actual occurrence of a **disease**, we say that such illnesses are biopsychosocial in origin.

WHO IS AT RISK?

Family History Predisposes Us

Given enough stress, virtually all of us are vulnerable to disease. But as I have discussed previously, we are more likely to contract one illness over another because of certain predispositions. Therefore, if you know that mood disorders, chemical dependency, or any form of mental illness run in your family, your children are

Bio-Psycho-Social Disease Model of Depression And Chemical Dependency

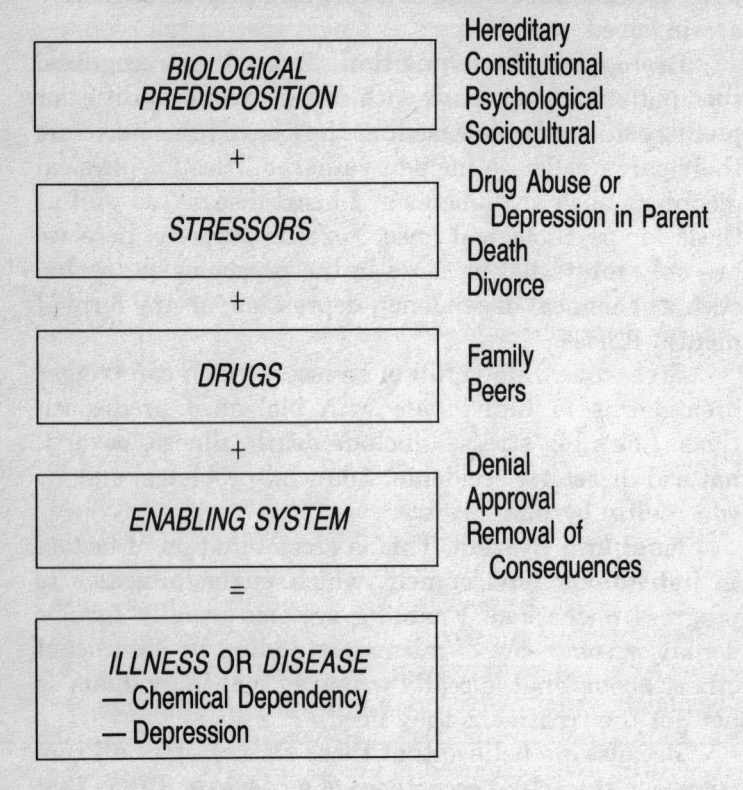

BIOLOGICAL PREDISPOSITION	Hereditary Constitutional Psychological Sociocultural
+	
STRESSORS	Drug Abuse or Depression in Parent Death Divorce
+	
DRUGS	Family Peers
+	
ENABLING SYSTEM	Denial Approval Removal of Consequences
=	
ILLNESS OR DISEASE — Chemical Dependency — Depression	

especially at risk for developing these conditions when divorce occurs.

Of course, you might not be aware that any of your relatives now has or has previously suffered from one or more of these disorders. Because of the denial involved and the misdiagnoses that so frequently occurs, many people don't even know they are chemically dependent or depressed. This is especially true of former generations. Family secrets and ignorance about the true nature of someone's peculiar ways are as old as time itself. So that aunt who was labeled an oddball or great-grandfather who could never seem to keep a job might both have been victims of either one of these disorders.

As far as outright mental illness such as schizophrenia is concerned, even in these modern time families still hide this disease from relatives because of the shame that they feel.

Incidence of Disorders High

Just remember that clinical depression is very common, affecting some 20 percent of the population. At present approximately 15 percent of Americans are believed to be in some stages of a chemical dependency.

Relationship between Depression and Manic Depression

Anyone who experiences a depressive episode is at risk for having a manic one as well, or for suffering from what is technically known as a bi-polar disorder. In the United States, depression and bi-polar illnesses are believed to mar the lives of as many as 16 million people. One out of three college students are likely to experience a depressive, manic, or bi-polar episode before graduating. In the freshman year alone, one out of five will have experienced depression.

Depression and Drug Use Connected

Depression and drug abuse often go hand in hand. Those who are depressed often turn to drink or drugs to ease their woes. Drugs of any kind can cause or exacerbate depression or any mental imbalance.

As a parent it is urgent that you realize how vulnerable you and your children are to chemical dependency, mood disorders, and other psychological illnesses, especially during the topsy-turvy times of divorce. You must be especially aware if either of these two disorders run in your family. Being sensitive to this should enable you to take appropriate measures before things get out of hand.

"Difficult" Children Another Vulnerable Group

In recent years, longitudinal studies have found that as many as 15 percent of all children are born with what are called "difficult" temperaments. The extreme of these are the hyperactive children who can't seem to sit still, frequently have learning disabilities, and are the source of much frustration for parents and teachers. The truly hyperactive are easy to spot and now can be treated with medication and special attention of some sort.

But there are many young people who are not so extreme yet fall into this category. Like the truly hyperactive, they are intense and exhibit many traits that make them hard to raise. These can include erratic eating and sleeping patterns, general "unhappiness," negative reactions to anything new, problems with transition and change, and loudness. These children can be of any intelligence level. Even if they are bright, they can have learning disabilities.

If learning disabilities are undetected and untreated, which is often the case, these young people can be set on a path of failure and frustration.

Because these "difficult" children are often not diagnosed correctly when small, they quickly become labeled as unmanageable, high-strung or even "bad" kids. This sets into motion a vicious cycle which often becomes a self-fulfilling prophecy, wherein their low self-esteem drives them into antisocial and self-destructive acts, reinforcing everyone's belief that they were no good to start with. As I mentioned at one point, these are often the children who become scapegoats in dysfunctional families, such as those in the throes of a divorce. As a result they can be at risk for developing more serious problems when their parents' marriage breaks down. A recent survey of our population at The Regent Hospital found that children from divorced families were twice as likely to have learning disorders as children from intact families.

If any of this sounds familiar, I strongly urge you to read the book *The Difficult Child* by Stanley Turecki, M.D., which discusses these children in detail and offers excellent advice on effective ways to deal with them.

DIVORCE KEY STRESSOR

As I have shown throughout this book, divorce is a major life stressor. As with death, illness, poverty, or any number of traumas, divorce can trigger breakdowns in the kinds of vulnerable individuals just described above. I have discussed in detail throughout this book all the many ways it can buffet both parents and children, leaving them exhausted and confused. Ideally, if individuals get the proper help and support they need early on, their illness has a chance of being halted before it progresses too far. But, as I mentioned above, there are often forces at work in their environments which keep that from happening. We call these forces enabling systems.

ENABLING SYSTEMS

When people have serious problems and those around them do things to take away the consequences of their behavior, we say that an enabling system is in effect. Such systems are very common in the families of the chemically dependent. Often when individuals with a drinking or drug problem start doing things that could get them into trouble—when they start missing work or school, for example—parents or spouses will cover for them, calling their boss or teacher and saying they are sick.

Not recognizing that people's unfavorable behavior

are symptoms of underlying problems also enables psychological illnesses to progress. Blaming, putting down, or punishing individuals when they start being difficult or doing undesirable things, instead of getting them the help that they need, invariably contributes to a downward spiral.

Enabling Systems During Divorce

Enabling systems often operate for young people who begin acting out or behaving strangely or out of character during a divorce. The fact families are so preoccupied with their own issues in itself enables children to progress in what at times becomes full-blown illnesses. Instead of addressing problems head-on, parents, teachers, and school counselors might underplay their importance until the behavior becomes too extreme to ignore. This is a form of denial. It is often the result of both ignorance and good intentions. People are just not equipped to discern that things are headed in a dangerous direction. And many adults feel it best to protect young people from what may seem like the too harsh consequences of their behavior. In my experience it often does more harm than good to minimize the seriousness of teens' and young adults' difficulties.

By the same token, overreacting to negative behavior can have unfortunate consequences also. If young people are labeled bad or troublesome and get punished severely or too often instead of getting the help they need, their self-esteem is usually damaged as a result. And as we have seen, low self-esteem is often at the root of much self-destructive or antisocial behavior.

From the above, I hope it is clear now to you how biological predispositions, stress, and enabling systems interact and result in distress if not outright illness for young people of divorce. Now I would like to focus in on specifics to help you unscramble what's going on with your sons or daughters and take effective action.

ACTING OUT REVISITED

As I described in Chapter 3, young people have not yet acquired the language necessary to express their feelings adequately. When upset or angry, instead of saying so directly, they frequently act them out behaviorally. The behavior itself serves as an outlet for the pain they might be feeling subconsciously and lessens its sting by allowing them to avoid thinking directly about what is bothering them. Adults, of course, do this also, but hopefully less often because of their greater maturity.

A divorce or the threat of a divorce can be profoundly upsetting and confusing for young people. So much so in fact that the emotional turmoil can be downright overwhelming. As a result, teens and young adults may start acting in ways that leave their parents perplexed. A formerly pleasant, compliant 13-year-old girl, might start talking back and acting hostile and totally uncooperative after her parents inform her about an impending divorce. An otherwise good student and good kid will suddenly start having trouble in school and with the law when his parents separate. Or an already high-strung or difficult teenager will begin acting bizarrely, exhibiting wild mood swings and sudden sloppiness in dress when her parents' battling begins taking on ominous tones.

WHAT TO LOOK FOR

The following are the most common ways young people will act out their anger or upset over your divorce:

- Aggressive behavior. Getting into fights with siblings or other children. Arguing and fighting with you, peers or anyone in authority. Actual physical aggression with anyone.
- General uncooperativeness, sullenness or hostility.

- Withdrawal from activity. Uncommunicativeness. Sadness. Breaking off with friends. Isolation and onset of clinical depression.
- School problems. Drop in grades, truancy, etc.
- Somatic complaints. These include headaches, stomachaches, and so on.
- Drastic changes in eating patterns—overeating, or extreme dieting. Onset of anorexia or bulimia under stress of divorce.
- Breaking the law. This can include such things as stealing, vandalism, disturbing the peace, wilding, and so on.
- Taking drugs or drinking. Abusing any substance.
- Sudden precocity in dress and appearance. Promiscuity.
- Staying out late at night or not coming home at all some nights. Running away.

NOT-SO-SERIOUS VS. SERIOUS

In their milder forms, most of these behaviors can be considered somewhat "normal" for teens and young adults experiencing a divorce. Argumentativeness, sadness and withdrawal, a drop in grades, changes in eating habits or physical complaints that don't last too long or become too extreme are common responses. If your teens or young adults exhibit several of these behaviors, if any of them start becoming extreme or continue on for more than a few months, you should be aware that they might be symptoms of an early disease process such as depression or chemical dependency.

This is especially so if mood disorders, alcoholism, or any other psychiatric illnesses have occurred in your immediate or extended family. If you have any doubts, you should seek professional advice for help in evaluating their problems and deciding what to do.

ANTISOCIAL BEHAVIOR

Any antisocial behavior—illegal activity, alcohol or drug taking, inappropriate sexual behavior, severe isolation, continued drop in grades—has to be viewed as serious symptoms. Because of their potential to get a young person into trouble which they might have to pay for for the rest of their lives, parents should not slough off these symptoms as minor or unimportant.

You should discuss these symptoms with your child and let them know you are concerned. Taking a sympathetic approach to the hurt and anger they may be feeling about the divorce is always advisable. If you begin to realize that you are not getting anywhere and the behavior does not improve, my advice to you is to seek out counseling. If things have progressed to the point that there is evidence of serious substance abuse, that your son or daughter has run away, is behaving promiscuously, or there is any hint of suicidal tendencies or self-mutilation, getting professional help is all the more crucial. In all instances, these behaviors are symptoms of the beginning stages of a serious psychiatric disorder and may be life-threatening.

WHEN IS DRINKING AND DRUG TAKING DANGEROUS?

Remember, alcohol and drugs impair judgment and loosen normal restraints, often drawing young people into dangerous territory. I believe it is extremely important to discourage your teens or young adults from experimenting at all. In New York State, for example, 80 percent of auto accidents have been found to be alcohol or drug related. A common theme in the new evidence on date rape is that one or both young people involved were under the influence of some kind of mood altering substance, again usually alcohol. And many a young person's plans for the future have been derailed by an unwanted pregnancy that could have been avoided if their good sense had not been clouded by drugs or alcohol.

Of course, if there is any history of substance abuse in your family, your offsprings' seemingly innocent experimentation might be the beginning of a dependency that could eventually wreak havoc on their lives and require intense treatment.

Addressing the problem head on, early on in the case is vital.

Warning Signs

The following are things that might indicate your teen or young adult has reached a dangerous point in their use of drugs or alcohol:

- Two or more clear instances of drug abuse. This includes any time you see them stoned, drunk, or high. Any time there is a suicide attempt involving drugs is also a real danger signal.
- Regular use of any drugs, especially after you've let them know your disapproval.
- Serious slippage in school grades or attendance.
- Worsening family relationships.
- Extreme, negative personality changes.
- Rundown state of health.
- Drug-culture attire.
- Run-ins with the law.
- Undesirable new friends.
- Suddenly needing or having more money.

WHEN IS DEPRESSION SERIOUS?

In common parlance, when we say we are depressed we mean we feel down, blue, or sad. Let's face it, we all get depressed sometimes. But a clinical depression is something else. As with many facets of behavior, it's a matter of degree in deciding what's normal from abnormal.

A true clinical depression is a prolonged state that lasts more than six to eight weeks. In this type of condition people have symptoms that include feeling down, hopelessness, experiencing a loss of energy, sense of direction, and initiative. Clinically depressed individuals might have difficulty going to sleep, they might sleep all of the time, or they might have trouble getting up in the morning. There can be a loss of appetite and weight, or the opposite. Often depressed individuals withdraw from others and tend to get isolated.

The seriously depressed person can also become hostile, negative, irritable and obnoxious. They can be argumentative and do a lot of blaming and putting others down.

If untreated, clinical depression can lead to obsessive thinking, rumination, worrying, indecisiveness, and suicide. In some individuals it can progress to psychotic behavior which includes hallucinations and delusions.

Suicidal Feelings

The most dangerous implication of depression for young people is that it can and often does result in suicidal feelings. These can show themselves in actual suicidal attempts or self-mutilation, such as cutting or burning of the skin.

If there is any indication of suicidal tendencies in your teen or young adult, get them into counseling immediately.

If they exhibit any of the other symptoms of a clinical depression for six to eight weeks they also need psychiatric counseling.

Manic Behavior

As I noted earlier, anyone who has had a depressive episode is at risk for experiencing a manic one as well. Manic acting out is the opposite of depressive behavior. Individuals might seem very happy and high, go on spending sprees, talk rapidly and make great plans. Their judgment is often impaired to the point that they make rash decisions and do intemperate things. If paranoid delusions are present, then the person is said to be psychotic.

Other Mental Illnesses

Though there are a great number of classifications of mental illness, it is not necessary for you to know them in any detail. Generally speaking, if your teens or young adults exhibit any of the following behavior you should be concerned and seek psychiatric help for them:

- Delusions and/or hallucinations.
- Ideas of persecution, that someone or something is out to get them with no realistic evidence to support this.
- Talking to themselves with any regularity, or not making sense when they speak.
- Irrational thoughts.
- Extreme withdrawal and incommunicativeness. Flatness or little expression of emotion.
- Any indication that they have taken on a new identity, thinking that they are someone else entirely.
- Extreme confusion or disorientation.
- Change in appearance that includes wild or very sloppy dress or generally disheveled appearance.
- Impaired performance at school.
- Severe withdrawal and decreased communication.

Chapter 6

Getting Help

There is almost nothing on earth as complex as the human body, with the exception, of course, of the human psyche and personality, and, it follows, our relationships with one another. Because of this, most of us have difficulty understanding ourselves and seeing ourselves objectively even under the best of circumstances. During crises, such as divorce, it is nearly impossible.

That's where modern psychiatry and psychology come in. For the past several decades, social scientists have been intensely studying human behavior in all its many facets.

The information and understanding they have compiled during that time is truly impressive. The benefit of this to all of us is that when we undergo any kind of trauma or breakdown we can avail ourselves of this new understanding by going to see a qualified counselor.

As I have attempted to make clear to you throughout this book, there are numerous complex forces at work that contribute to the breakdown of marriages which affect all family members. Understanding this can be very helpful when you are in the midst of the whirlwind that divorce inevitably is. But understanding is often not enough. The forces can be so strong that you can still get buffeted about and knocked down if you try to plow through on your own.

That is why I have continually stressed the importance of getting help early on. By the same token, I urge you to seek professional help if anyone in your family has gotten to the point of actual psychiatric illness, be it depression, chemical dependency, or any one of a number of disorders. If either depression or chemical dependency—or both—are present, young people's very lives can be at risk.

GETTING HELP MAY BE LIFE-OR-DEATH ISSUE

I say this because the death rate for young people between the ages of 15 and 25 has increased a startling 30 percent in the last ten years. The main causes for these deaths are suicide, accidents, and homicide. We know that mood disorders are present in some 30 to 45 percent of those who successfully attempt suicide. The San Diego study showed that as many as 75 percent of suicide victims had previously been diagnosed as substance abusers. We are that aware that drugs and alcohol play a significant part in automobile accidents. And as I have demonstrated throughout this book, depression and chemical dependency not only can contribute to divorce but can be exacerbated by divorce.

Such clear-cut interrelationships between these factors make a compelling case for families of divorce to get appropriate help for themselves and for their children. To aid you in this process, I will devote this chapter to reviewing the different therapies and treatments available, discussing when you might need each one of them, and offering guidelines for selecting the right therapist for you and on deciding when inpatient treatment might be indicated. I will also describe the program at The Regent Hospital to give you an idea of what to expect should inpatient treatment ever be necessary for your troubled adolescent or young adult.

WHAT IS THERAPY?

When you are physically ill, you go to a doctor for treatment because you know that you are unable to treat yourself. The human body is an awesomely complex creation and requires a true specialist to fix it when it breaks down. The same holds true for our psychological and emotional selves. When things start to go seriously wrong in our lives, as in the case of divorce or the breakdown of one of our family members, most of us are just not equipped to set things right on our own.

Psychologists, social workers, and psychiatrists have spent years studying human behavior in order to treat people in times of personal crisis. Therapy is essentially a learning process whereby we, as mental health professionals, help individuals to understand the forces that drive people to behave in certain ways, to see what they are doing that might be harmful to themselves and others, and to suggest constructive alternatives so that they can function more satisfactorily. If they have a diagnosable psychiatric disorder, we might treat them with medication or a whole range of specific therapies.

Throughout this book, I have tried to offer guidelines for deciding when outside help is necessary. Now I would like to explain what your options are in this regard.

MARRIAGE COUNSELING

Oftentimes a family's first experience with therapy will be in the early stages of a couple's problems. An experienced marital counselor should be able to hone in on those issues which are dividing you and to give you constructive ways to resolve your differences. They should be able to help you decide whether or not your marriage can be saved, and if not, what steps you can take to handle your divorce in the most amicable fashion possible. They can also make recommendations if family or individual therapy is indicated for any family member.

FAMILY THERAPY

Family therapy is based on the notion that a family, much like the human body itself, is a system of interdependent parts. The family's function is to see to it that all members thrive and are able to carry out their appropriate tasks. Parents' tasks include nurturing and providing a safe environment for their children. Children's tasks are to grow and develop so that they may one day attain independence and perhaps start families of their own. Ideally, when all members are playing their parts as they should, the family hums along smoothly like a well-oiled machine.

During times of stress, the delicate balance of the family system goes out of kilter. As with the body, when one part breaks down, others have to work overtime to keep the whole system from faltering. If the relationship between the key players—that is, the marital relationship itself—begins to come apart, other members of the system are going to show signs of distress. Because the main tasks of the family become disrupted at these times, we say that it is dysfunctional.

In dysfunctional families, to redress the balance different members often assume roles that ultimately turn out to be harmful to themselves. As I described in earlier chapters, one parent might become a "super" parent to make up for the other's deficiencies and exhaust him or herself in the process. Or one child might take on the role of the scapegoat, acting as both a symptom of and safety valve for all that is wrong within the family. If that person is brought in for treatment, they often cannot get well unless the whole family is seen and the system's unhealthy patterns are altered. Or if one person does get well through treatment or other means, oftentimes different members take turns at being the "sick" one again, until the underlying problems of the larger system itself are rectified. Since people who come from dysfunctional families tend to reenact the same patterns in their own families when they become adults, it is very important for them to have these things pointed out so that they can free themselves from continuing unhealthy practices.

DYSFUNCTIONAL FAMILY

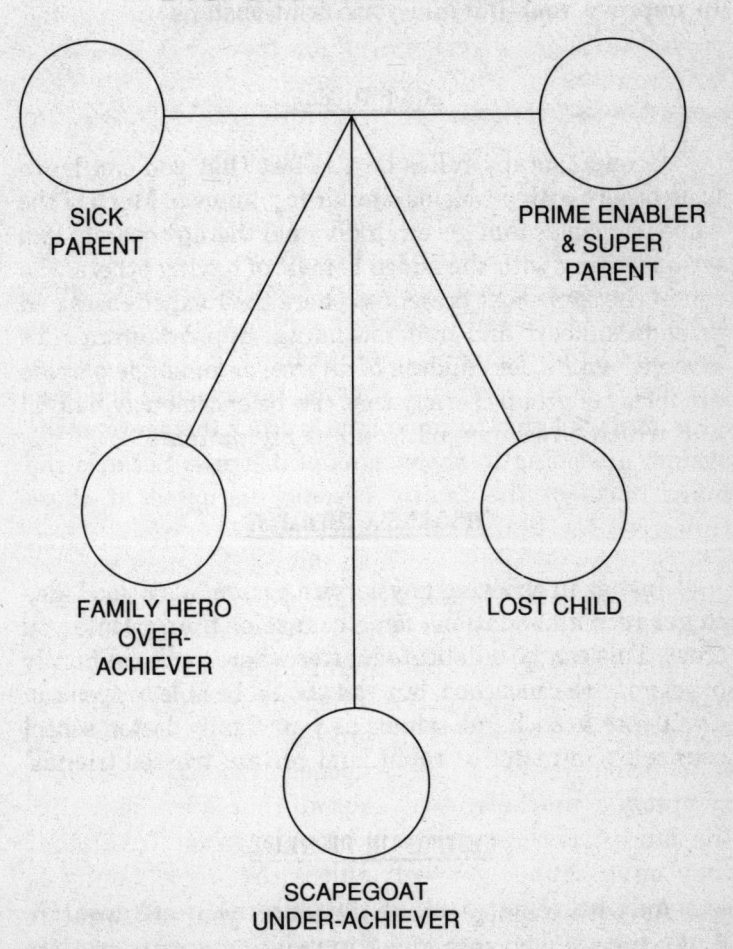

SICK PARENT

PRIME ENABLER & SUPER PARENT

FAMILY HERO OVER-ACHIEVER

LOST CHILD

SCAPEGOAT UNDER-ACHIEVER

INDIVIDUAL COUNSELING

Here an individual's specific problems are addressed in depth. If you or any members of your family are showing real signs of emotional or psychological disturbance as the result of your divorce, talking it over with a qualified therapist is often the first step toward getting back in balance. This person should be able to treat specific disorders as well as to help you understand what it is you are going through and what steps you can take to improve your life and your relationships.

GROUP THERAPY

Group therapy relies on the fact that you can learn from others with problems similar to your own. Much of the same principles that govern individual therapy operate in a group setting with the added benefit of having others who are in the same boat present to share their experiences and provide support and understanding. Support groups for divorced adults, for children of divorce, or for single parents are forms of group therapy that can be enormously helpful and which I recommend to all of my patients.

CHOOSING A THERAPIST

Just as in choosing any service person, it's a good idea to get recommendations for a counselor from people you trust. This can be a delicate matter where personal family problems are concerned, but you should be able to speak in confidence to such individuals as your family doctor, school counselor, minister or rabbi, and certain trusted friends.

GETTING THE RIGHT FIT

As with most physical ailments, you will want to find someone who specializes in treating your particular problem. If your marital relationship is hurting, seek out individuals who have experience in treating couples. If you suspect that there are unhealthy patterns in your family as I have described previously, a qualified family therapist will be most suitable for your needs. If you or one of your family members is showing signs of real distress, individual therapy might be in order. By the same token, if you or a family member are suffering from either chemical dependency or depression, it is imperative to select a therapist who has direct experience and training in treating these disorders. Any responsible practitioner qualified in any of these specialties should be able to tell you if any of the other types of therapies are indicated for you and your family.

IS THIS THE RIGHT THERAPIST FOR YOU?

Even after getting a wonderful recommendation, sometimes you might end up with someone who doesn't seem right somehow. A good rule of thumb here is to trust your instincts. By its very nature, therapy will make you uncomfortable. But in the initial stages, you should feel trust, respect and liking for the person if the relationship is ever to be fruitful. If after a few sessions, you just don't feel compatible with your therapist, look around for someone else. If this continues to happen after seeing several individuals, you should start suspecting that your expectations might be unrealistic. At that point it is a good idea to review in your mind everyone you have seen so far, choose the best one and give it a shot.

HOW TO TELL IF IT'S WORKING

Very early on in the process, your therapist should be able to tell you what your problem is—i.e., to give you a diagnosis. Another important part of the therapist's job is to outline objectives for you and assign concrete things that you should be working on during your time together. These could include a better way to manage you anger, how to handle your depression or your ambivalent feelings for your sick child.

Though at first you are likely to feel worse because of the sensitive issues that are being addressed, over time— say, a period of six months or so—things should improve. You should be gaining clarity about what is going on in your life. You should have learned more effective ways to handle your problems and be better prepared to deal with new ones as they arise. If these things are not occurring, perhaps you should look for someone else to help you out. There is no sense wasting your precious time and money if you are not getting results.

WHEN INPATIENT TREATMENT IS INDICATED

When in the early stages of any psychological disturbance, most individuals can and should be treated on an outpatient basis. But when illnesses progress to the point that individuals' whole lives are being affected and may in fact be in danger, inpatient programs are the only solution. Just as a doctor wouldn't try to treat someone who is hemorrhaging in a clinic, so your therapist should not try to treat anyone as an outpatient if he or she is at the point of total dysfunction. This could mean a youngster who is being verbally aggressive, is running away, stealing, and being truant from school. It could mean a teen or young adult who is doing drugs, has given any indication of suicidal thoughts or has gotten into trouble with the law. Or it could mean a spouse whose chemical dependency has progressed to the point that he or she can't go to work or take care of young children, and so forth.

The purpose of inpatient treatment at such times is to put individuals in a safe environment, to stop the destructive acting out, and to get an accurate diagnosis so that the appropriate treatment can begin. Before entering any program, you should make sure that staff there intend to give you a specific diagnosis and a concrete plan of action very early on. Those that don't do this are usually not very helpful and should be avoided.

Though many people resist the notion of inpatient treatment because of the trauma and stigma it can bring, it is critical to recognize when it is necessary. Hesitating too long often results in unnecessarily dire consequences, such as jail sentences or even death.

THE REGENT HOSPITAL

Most inpatient programs available today are designed to treat either straight psychiatric disorders, chemical dependency or what is known as dual-diagnosis disorders. Dual diagnostic programs are a relatively new entity which emerged in the last ten years. They reflect the growing awareness that individuals often suffer from a combination of disturbances, as I have discussed previously, which need to be teased out and each treated in an appropriate manner if the individual is to be truly rehabilitated.

The program at The Regent Hospital, known as The Foundry, qualifies as a dual diagnostic treatment program, though in fact it is equipped to treat individuals suffering from three or more different psychiatric disorders. The most common combinations of these disorders are chemical dependency and mood disorders. These two frequently occur with learning disabilities and/or attention deficit disorder. We are also geared to help individuals with such problems as eating disorders and schizophrenic illness.

The Foundry is a very carefully structured therapeutic community that has four levels through which an individual must progress in order to complete the treatment.

The first ten days in the program are a time for evaluation, during which psychological, neuropsychiatric, and physiological tests (including drug screenings and biochemical tests for depression) are administered, interviews are conducted, and behavior is observed to determine the true nature of the problem. At the end of that time, a conference is held with the family and referring counselor or therapist to inform everyone of the diagnosis and treatment plans. If medications are needed they are recommended at this time.

Everyone enters the program at Level I, during which they do not have any privileges, such as leaving the premises or having family visitors only and supervised phone calls are to family members only. After the first week, if all of the rules have been followed, an individual has attended all therapy sessions, and so on, they are graduated to Level II, which allows them greater freedom and responsibility. This can include having visitors and taking supervised visits home or going on outings with the rest of the community and staff.

One of the goals in Level II is that participants learn to talk about their feelings instead of acting them out. When they demonstrate their success at this and comply with all the rules, they can then move onto Level III, where the task is to work on issues specific to their lives and particular disorder or set of disorders. The whole community votes to decide if members are ready to move to the next level.

At The Regent Hospital, we call the different treatment modalities tracks. If someone had a learning disability, we say they are on the learning disabilities track, attending groups and addressing issues that specifically deal with this problem. The same holds true if they are chemically dependent, suffer from a mood disorder or eating disorder, or have been physically or sexually abused.

Group, individual and family therapy sessions are conducted by a fully trained staff of psychiatrists, Ph.D. psychologists, CSW social workers, and CAC alcohol and drug abuse counselors. Each treatment program is tailored and updated weekly to meet each participant's needs.

Participants are seen by a psychiatrist on a daily

basis, who keeps a constant eye on their progress and prescribes and reviews medication when indicated. Each has an individual therapist and a case manager who oversees their case from beginning to end. Families are met with at least once a week and are also urged to attend a family program where they are seen both with and without their children present to discuss pertinent issues. We work closely with the family to ensure that important family problems are addressed and that discharge plans will be successful.

HOLISTIC APPROACH

Because we take a holistic view of treating troubled young people, we provide workshops in such things as karate, yoga, music, and art, and we encourage them to learn how to have "sober" fun by planning trips to museums and movies on a regular basis. We also do vocational counseling to help our teens and young adults discover their talents and to steer them into constructive lines of work.

AFTER DISCHARGE

The average length of stay in The Foundry is 60 days. After discharge, we encourage participants to join our alumni group which has many activities and allows them to hook up with peers who are doing wholesome things together. This is a very popular program and staff often come along on their outings, which include ice-skating parties or an evening of such activities as billiards and dancing. This is all part of our commitment to teach young people—who many times have never really learned before—how to live healthy, sober, fulfilling lives.

Chapter 7

Your Changing Relationship

THE ROCKY WATERS OF PARENT/TEEN RELATIONSHIPS

Mary, a 35-year-old divorced secretary, talks about her teenaged son:

> It was difficult enough dealing with John before the divorce. He was going through the stage where he seemed to feel the need to test me all of the time. Since the divorce, he has become impossible. He's either outright hostile or sullen. I just don't know what to do about it.

Tom, a 40-year-old construction worker whose wife has left him with custody of his 16-year-old daughter, worries about her:

> I'm really confused about how to deal with Melissa. She was always happy and fun to be with, but that's all changed now. First she's up, then she's down. She used to be so thoughtful and responsible. But since the divorce she's gone through a real personality change. Her room is a mess and I don't like how she's dressing these days. We seem to fight about everything and I'm at a loss about what to do.

Sound familiar? Adolescence can be a tough time for parents and young people even in the best of times. During a divorce good relations can seem downright impossible. My purpose in this chapter is to give you a better understanding of all the forces at work between you and your teens and young adults amidst these rocky times with the ultimate aim of making things go more smoothly for all involved.

THE TERRIBLE TEENS

As I outlined in Chapter 3, from about the ages of 10 or 11 through the early 20s, young people undergo enormous physical, psychological, and behavioral changes that puts them off-balance and makes them very vulnerable to stress. It also can make them very hard to live with. Knowing this can help you to be a more sympathetic and effective parent. Understanding yourself and your own reactions is important too.

PARENTS' ROLE IN POOR RELATIONSHIPS

The whole thrust toward independence and differentiation from you which characterizes this time of your children's lives can be very threatening. Adolescence signals the beginning of the end of their total dependence on you. Sometimes it seems that they must question and reject just about everything you have tried to teach them. Sometimes it seems that they hold little respect for you or any of your values. If you are like many people, you will probably find this all a little hard to take. You might even experience a real sense of grief at the loss of so many pleasurable aspects of your parental role and of your relationship with your children.

Seeing your children start to blossom into early adulthood can stimulate pleasant as well as unpleasant memories of your own youth. Old unresolved conflicts and identity issues that were long ago buried can surface and bring you discomfort. Your children's budding maturity can also arouse such untoward and perhaps surprising feelings as envy of their emerging sexuality or a sense of competitiveness with their new-found knowledge of life and of the world.

If your children's adolescence coincides with your own midlife, you might be experiencing fragmentation and a lack of vigor in your own sense of yourself. This naturally makes any challenges from your offspring all the more threatening.

Of course, all of these mixed feelings are added into the normal ambivalence that you might have felt for years about being a parent in the first place. As I mentioned in Chapter 1, you might harbor some resentment toward your children for the great burden they represent in your life. You might have had them when you were too young. Your marriage might have changed for the worse since they have been born. You might have been deprived of proper nurturing and good parenting yourself and have been left somewhat emotionally damaged as a result. And so on.

At the same time, your adolescents are experiencing a whole host of their own confusing emotions about themselves, about you, and about life in general.

UNDERSTANDING AND HUMOR THE KEYS

How, you might ask, do parents and young people ever get along? In my view, adults must have a clear understanding of what their children and they themselves are going through in order to sail through these years with any amount of equanimity. A good sense of humor helps an awful lot, too.

DIVORCE CAN TIP THE BALANCE

Add a divorce into the bubbling cauldron of mixed emotions that exist between many parents and their adolescents, and you have a recipe almost guaranteed to boil over into trouble.

When you get a divorce, you are unleashing the forces to set into motion your own identity crisis. As I discussed in earlier chapters, your self-esteem can start to crumble. Feelings of failure about your marriage and fears for your future can seriously undermine your self-confidence.

Though parenting normally requires a good deal of self-sacrifice, your own narcissistic needs at the time of divorce can seem more important than those of your children.

FROM YOUR CHILDREN'S PERSPECTIVE

Sarah, 19, voices a typical view of children of divorce:

> Not only had I lost my dad, but I felt like I lost my mother too. She was hardly home any more, and when she was there she was too tired to do anything. It makes me sad, but it makes me real angry, too, to have lost so much.

Fourteen-year-old Barbara's solution to her parents' divorce is all too typical of many adolescents:

> Mom was so depressed all of the time, that I felt I had to do everything possible to keep her going. I gave up seeing my friends just to be with her. I'm scared about not having enough money anymore. And I'm even more scared that she might fall apart.

Divorce, as you can see from the above quotes and as I have discussed at length previously, arouses all kinds of fears and anxieties in your children. If you are preoccupied, they may cling to you or demand more attention than normal. If you turn to them for comfort, you may feel guilty about this.

Adolescents and young adults usually feel a good deal of anger when their parents divorce. They might express this directly or act it out in any number of antisocial and unappealing ways. They might also show it by being downright obnoxious to your new beau or mate.

If they start to have serious problems, such as I have discussed in detail in Chapter 5, this adds to your sense of fear, helplessness and panic.

YOU ALL CAN SURVIVE IT

Understanding what you and your offspring are going through is a major step in mitigating the negative effects of divorce. No matter how badly they are behaving and how conflicted and overwhelmed you feel, sympathy on your part instead of blame can do wonders for all. You can show this sympathy by keeping communication as open as possible between you and your adolescents or young adults.

If they are having serious behavior problems, it's important that you let them know that you still love them and are in their corner. Your estimation of them is crucial to their self-esteem and their ultimate good mental health as an adult.

PARENTS FOR LIFE

Though you can divorce your spouse and end your marriage, you can never stop being your children's parents. Even if you move away and never see them again, even if you die, you will still loom large in their hearts and minds for their entire lives. Most of us have children without fully realizing this, or without being aware that parenting is probably the biggest responsibility and most serious undertaking we will have in our lives.

Even if we feel ambivalence or open resentment toward our children, all but the most hard-hearted or emotionally damaged individuals among us want to be good and responsible parents. Though this becomes especially difficult during a divorce, there are many things you can do to continue your parenting role in a helpful and loving manner.

DAY-TO-DAY CONCERNS

For Mothers

Ninety percent of young people stay with their mothers after a divorce. Consequently, it is the mother who assumes the biggest responsibility and burden of single parenting.

Studies have shown that the mental health and quality of the parenting of the mother is the single most important factor in the overall adjustment of children to divorce. Needless to say, this makes it very important for mothers to do everything they can to get the support they need to raise their children. That is why you should not take it lightly when I advise you to get help for yourself when the role of single parenting becomes too much to handle.

Super Mom Overwhelming

Without the help of a mate, many women take on the role of super parent, acting as breadwinner, disciplinarian, and nurturer. It is the rare person who can carry this on without feeling some resentment and outright exhaustion.

Fathers Can Share Burden

Keeping the children's father in the picture means that you can have much-needed help in sharing the burden of parenting. Needless to say, this is all the more reason to go out of your way to develop an amicable relationship with your ex-spouse. If this is not possible, you can get a good deal of bolstering and understanding by joining a support group for single parents.

Adolescents, especially boys, need a father or someone who will take on that role to help them with important identity tasks. If your ex just can't be all that involved, you should try to enlist an uncle, close friend, or even a counselor. If this is not possible, have your son join a scouting group or look into the Big Brothers association in your area.

For Fathers

As I noted above, in the vast majority of cases mothers are the ones who get custody of the children. Being a part-time parent can be devastating for many men. If you are affected this way, I strongly advise counseling to help you work through your normal feelings of sadness and loss.

Not having a father present can be very hard for children also. Adolescence in particular is a time when both girls and boys need a father present to help them through specific identity tasks and to separate from their mothers.

Stay in Their Lives

In her excellent book *Second Chances,* which reports on the results of a longitudinal study of children of divorce, psychologist Judith Wallerstein tells how after the first few years many fathers have very limited contact with their children and some none at all. She gives touching quotes which testify to the fact that these children often mourn their missing fathers for years and are at risk of going through life vainly searching for that part of themselves which is missing as a result. Don't underestimate how important you are as a father to your children. Maintaining a good relationship with them after the divorce can have far-reaching benefits for both you and them.

Financial Support Essential

After divorce, all too many absent fathers relinquish their financial responsibilities to their former spouses and children, being late or just not paying much-needed support contributions. This places an enormous and unfair burden on single mothers, often plunging them into near or actual poverty and making life extra difficult for everyone involved.

In *Second Chances* Dr. Wallerstein also mentions the phenomenon of fathers cutting off aid the minute their children reach 18. Though this may be justified under law, in reality it can make things very tough for the young people themselves. Teens and young adults are often deprived of a college education or technical training, which after all is their birthright in this country, because their fathers refuse to pay for it after a divorce. I strongly advise all fathers and mothers who can afford to do so to do everything possible to provide their sons and daughters with the education and training they need to survive in this competitive world. This is especially true if they are children of divorce and are already facing life with a definite handicap.

Single Fathers

If you are one of the rare fathers who has custody of your children, be sure to take care that single parenting does not overwhelm you also. As the sole parent of your children, your mental health is crucial to their good adjustment. Single parent support groups are available for you as well as women and there is much to be gained by joining one when things get tough.

For Both Parents

If you must work more than before or go back to school, put aside time to be with your children for fun or serious talk. When and if you start dating, make sure that that time remains sacrosanct between you and them without the presence of your new love interest.

Structure, Routine, and Supervision Important

The academic and behavior problems of children of divorce can result from the fact that parents just don't spend the time with them that they formerly did. That's why it's important to try to remain as involved as possible with your adolescents and young adults, and to keep structure and order in their daily routines. Continue to review their homework, and to supervise and regulate such things as television watching, bedtime, time out with friends, and so on.

Good Relationship with Ex

Do everything possible to maintain an amicable relationship with your former spouse, for all the many reasons I have cited throughout this book. If your ex-spouse is a reasonable person whose presence does not harm your children, try to keep him or her involved in your children's lives as much as possible. Even though you may remarry and your children might be fond of your new mate, they still need and want contact with their biological parent.

Suppose your ex-spouse is completely uncooperative, argumentative, divisive, or even violent? My advice to you in this case is to seek professional assistance in helping you to work out the best way to deal with such an intractable individual.

Read and put into practice all of the advice at the end of the last chapter on ways to reduce parental warfare.

Keep Your Ambivalence to Yourself

Even if you have ambivalent feelings about your children, try not to communicate them. Though it may seem harmless and even honest to do this, children are very sensitive and can be deeply wounded by such admissions from their parents. I have patients whose parents let them know repeatedly that their lives are harder because of them. The pain these young people feel is profound and long-lasting.

Go Slow With New Relationships

Go slow with dating and remarriage after your divorce. Respect the fact that feelings are living, powerful forces that cannot be turned off overnight; by the same token new ones for new people usually don't materialize instantaneously but need a reasonable passage of time to take root and grow.

As I have stressed before, no matter how badly a parent might have behaved, children usually still feel love and loyalty for him or her. Bringing a new person into the picture arouses all kinds of intense and painful emotions in teens and young adults. It is best not to even bring your new love interests home until you are sure that you are serious. Even then, it is always advisable to be very discreet about displays of affection or any hint of a sexual relationship between you.

When you do remarry, your new mate should just work at being a friend to your children for a very long time before assuming the delicate role of a new parent.

MANAGING A TRUST FUND

Though you have severed your marriage ties with your spouse, you will always have one thing in common for life, and that is your children. I often ask my clients to view their mutual handling of their offspring after a divorce as though they were managing a trust fund. Doing this helps parents to put their children's needs before their own. The term for this role is coparenting.

I see many people making selfish decisions about such things as careers and new relationships after their marriage dissolves without any concerns for the effect it will have on their adolescents and young adults. As a result they might move to another part of the country and see them once a year, or bounce their children back and forth at will between households without even considering how hurtful this can be. Years later they look back in regret, wondering what went wrong.

INVESTING WISELY PAYS OFF FOR EVERYONE

This is less likely to happen if you realize that you have an investment in how your offspring turn out. If you manage things well and your children turn out okay despite your divorce, the rewards will be great indeed. Remember parenting provides opportunities for individual growth that exist in few other areas of life. To do a decent job of raising your children is to make an investment in yourself as well.

Sources

Ahrons, Constance R., and Rodgers, Roy H., *Divorced Families*. New York: W. W. Norton & Company, 1987.

Aro, Hillevi, "Parental Discord, Divorce and Adolescent Development," *European Archives of Psychiatry and Neurological Sciences,* vol. 237 (1988), pp. 106–11.

Block, Jack; Block, Jeanne H., and Gjerde, Per F., "Parental Functioning and the Home Environment in Families of Divorce: Prospective and Concurrent Analysis," *Journal of the American Academy of Child and Adolescent Psychiatry,* 27: 2 (1988), pp. 207–13.

Breault, K.D., and Kposowa, Augustine J., "Explaining Divorce in the United States: A Study of 3,111 Counties, 1980," *Journal of Marriage and the Family,* vol. 49, (August 1987), pp. 549–58.

Burnside, Mary A.; Baer, Paul E.; McLaughlin, Robert J., and Pokorny, Alex D., "Alcohol Use by Adolescents in Disrupted Families," *Alcoholism: Clinical and Experimental Research,* (May, June 1986) vol. 10, pp. 274–78.

Camara, Kathleen A., and Resnick, Gary, "Styles of Conflict Resolution and Cooperation between Divorced Parents: Effects on Child Behavior and Adjustment," *American Journal of Orthopsychiatry,* 59: No. 4, (October 1989), pp. 560–75.

Chiroboga, David; Catron, Linda, and Weiler, Phillip, "Childhood Stress and Adult Functioning During Marital Separation," *Family Relations,* vol. 36 (1987), pp. 163–67.

Counts, Robert M., and Sacks, Anita, "The Need for Crisis Intervention During Marital Separation," *Social Work,* March–April 1985, pp. 146–50.

Dadds, M. R., "Families and the Origins of Child Behavior Problems," *Family Process,* vol. 26, (1987), pp. 341–57. As cited in Reid, William J., and Crisafulli, Alida, "Marital Discord and Child Behavior Problems: A Meta-Analysis," 18:1 (1990), pp. 105–17.

Demo, David H., and Acock, Alan C., "The Impact of Divorce on Children," *Journal of Marriage and the Family,* vol. 50 (August 1988), pp. 619–48.

Derdeyn, A.P., and Waters, D. B., "Parents and Adolescents: Empathy and the Vicissitudes of Development." In Feinstein, S.C., and Giovacchini, P. (eds.), *Adolescent Psychiatry*, vol. 5. New York: Jason Aronson, 1977, pp. 175–85. As cited in Lohr, Rebecca, "Divorced Parents and Adolescent Girls: The Bouncing Ball," *Clinical Social Work Journal*, 16:2 (Summer 1988), pp. 180–93.

Edwards, John N., "Changing Family Structures and Youthful Well-Being: Assessing the Future," *Journal of Family Issues*, vol. 8, pp. 355–72. As cited in Demo, David H., and Acock, Alan C., "The Impact of Divorce on Children," *Journal of Marriage and the Family*, vol. 50 (August 1988), pp. 619–48.

Elkind, David, *The Hurried Child*, rev. ed; Reading, Mass: Addison-Wesley, 1988.

Elson, M., "Parenthood and the Transformation of Narcissism in Parenthood." In Cohen, R.; Cohler, B., and Weissman, S., (eds.), *Parenthood: A Psychodynamic Perspective*. New York: Guilford Press, 1984, pp. 297–314. As cited in Lohr, Rebecca, "Divorced Parents and Adolescent Girls: The Bouncing Ball," *Clinical Social Work Journal*, 16: 2 (Summer 1988), pp. 180–93.

Emery, R.E., "Interparental Conflict and the Children of Discord and Divorce," *Psychological Bulletin*, vol. 92 (1982), pp. 310–30. As cited in Camara, Kathleen A., and Resnick, Gary, "Styles of Conflict Resolution and Cooperation Between Divorced Parents: Effects on Child Behavior and Adjustment," *American Journal of Orthopsychiatry*, 59:4 (1989), pp. 560–75.

———, "Interpersonal Conflict and the Children of Discord and Divorce." In: Olson, D.H., and Miller, B.C., (eds.), *Family Studies Review Yearbook*, vol. 2. Beverly Hills, Calif.: Sage, 1984, pp. 310–30. As cited in Reid, William J., and Crisafulli, Alida, "Marital Discord and Child Behavior Problems: A Meta-Analysis," 18:1 (1990), pp. 105–17.

Forehand, Rex, and McCombs, Amanda, "The Nature of Interparental Conflict of Married and Divorced Parents: Implications for Young Adolescents," *Journal of Abnormal Child Psychology*, 17:2 (1989), pp. 235–49.

———; McCombs, Amanda; Long, Nicholas; Brody, Gene, and Fauber, Robert, "Early Adolescent Adjustment to Recent Parental Divorce: The Role of Interparental Conflict and Adolescent Sex as Mediating Variables," *Journal of Consulting and Clinical Psychology*, 56:4 (1988), pp. 624–27.

Furstenberg, Frank F., Jr.; Morgan, S. Philip, and Allison, Paul D., "Paternal Participation and Children's Well-Being After Marital Dissolution," *American Sociological Review*, vol. 52 (1987), pp. 695–701.

Glenn, Norval D., and Kramer, Kathryn B., "The Psychological Well-Being of Adult Children of Divorce," *Journal of Marriage and the Family*, November 1985, pp. 905–12.

Glick, P.C., and Lin, Sung-Lin, "Recent Changes in Divorce and Remarriage," *Journal of Marriage and the Family*, as cited in Glick, P.C., "Marriage, Divorce and Living Arrangements: Prospective Changes," *Journal of Family Issues*, vol. 5 (1984), pp. 7–26. As cited in Visher, Emily B., and Visher, John S., "Parenting Coalitions After Remarriage: Dynamics and Therapeutic Guidelines," *Family Relations*, vol. 38 (1989), pp. 68–70.

Gold, Mark S., *The Good News About Depression*. New York: Bantam Books, 1986.

Guidubaldi, John; Cleminshaw, Helen K.; Perry, Joseph D.; Nastasi, Lightel, Jeannine, "The Role of Selected Family Environment Factors in

Children's Post-Divorce Adjustment," *Family Relations,* vol. 35 (January 1986), pp. 141-51.

Henricks, Lorraine, *Kids Who Do/Kids Who Don't. A Parent's Guide to Teens and Drugs.* Summit, N.J.: PIA Press, 1989.

Jacobson, Doris S., "The Impact of Marital Separation/ Divorce on Children: II. Interparent Hostility and Child Adjustment," *Journal of Divorce,* vol. 2 (1978), pp. 3–19. As cited in Demo, David H., and Acock, Alan C., "The Impact of Divorce on Children," *Journal of Marriage and the Family,* vol. 50 (August 1988), pp. 619–48.

Johnson, Coleen Leahy, "Socially Controlled Civility," *American Behavioral Scientist,* vol. 31 (July/August 1988), pp. 685–701.

Kalter, Neil, *Growing Up With Divorce.* New York: The Free Press, 1990.

Keith, Verna M., and Finlay, Barbara, "The Impact of Parental Divorce on Children's Educational Attainment, Marital Timing, and Likelihood of Divorce," *Journal of Marriage and the Family,* vol. 50 (August 1988), pp. 797–809.

Kinard, E. Milling, and Reinherz, Helen, "Effects of Marital Disruption on Children's School Aptitude and Achievement," *Journal of Marriage and the Family,* vol. 48 (May 1986), pp. 285–93.

Lewis, Robert, "Bringing Up a Generation of Stepchildren," *Trenton Times,* February 26, 1990.

Lyon, Eleanor; Silverman, Marsha L.; Howe, George W.; Bishop, Gerrie, and Armstrong, Bonita, "Stages of Divorce: Implications for Service Delivery," *The Journal of Contemporary Social Work,* May 1985, pp. 259–67.

Maccoby, Eleanor E.; Depner, Charlene E., and Mnookin, Robert H., "Coparenting in the Second year After Divorce," *Journal of Marriage and the Family,* vol. 52 (February 1990), pp. 141–55.

Margolin, G., "The Reciprocal Relationship Between Marital and Child Problems." In: Vincent, J.P., (ed.), *Advances in Family Intervention, Assessment and Theory.* Greenwich, Conn.: JAI Press, 1981, pp. 131–82. As cited in Reid, William J., and Crisafulli, Alida, "Marital Discord and Child Behavior Problems: A Meta-Analysis," *Journal of Abnormal Psychology,* 18:1 (1990), pp. 105–117.

Martin, Teresa Castro, and Bumpass, Larry L., "Recent Trends in Marital Disruption," *Demography,* 26:1 (February 1989), pp. 37–51.

McCarthy, J., "A Comparison of the Probability of the Dissolution of First and Second Marriages," *Demography,* vol. 15 (1978), pp. 345–59. As cited in Martin, Teresa Castro, and Bumpass, Larry L., "Recent Trends in Marital Disruption," *Demography,* 26:1 (February 1989), pp. 37–50.

McCloughlin, David, and Whitfield, Richard, "Adolescents and Their Experience of Parental Divorce," *Journal of Adolescence,* vol. 7 (1984), pp. 155–70.

McCombe, Amanda, and Forehand, Rex, "Adolescent School Performance Following Parental Divorce: Are There Family Factors That Can Enhance Success?" *Adolescence,* 29:96 (Winter 1989), pp. 871–80.

Merikangas, Kathleen Ries, "Divorce and Assortive Mating Among Depressed Patients," *American Journal of Psychiatry,* vol. 141 (1984), pp. 74–76.

Needle, Richard H.; Su, S. Susan, and Doherty, William J., "Divorce, Remarriage, and Adolescent Substance Use: A Prospective Longitudinal Study," *Journal of Marriage and the Family,* vol. 52 (February 1990), pp. 157–69.

Nicholas, Patricia, "Women Working and Divorce. Cause or effect?" *Psychology Today,* October 12, 1986.

Norton, Arthur J., and Moorman, Jeanne E., "Current Trends in Marriage and Divorce Among American Women," *Journal of Marriage and the Family,* vol. 49 (February 1987), pp. 3–14.

O'Leary, K.D., and Emery, R.D., "Marital Discord and Child Behavior Problems," In Levine, M.D., and Satz, P., (eds.), *Middle Childhood: Development and Dysfunction.* Baltimore: University Park Press, 1984, pp. 345–63. As cited in Reid, William J., and Crisafulli, Alida, "Marital Discord and Child Behavior Problems: A Meta-Analysis," *Journal of Abnormal Psychology,* 18:1 (1990), pp. 105–17.

———, "Marital Discord and Children: Problems, Strategies, Methodologies, and Results." In: Doyle, A.; Gold, D., and Moskowitz, D.S., (eds.), *Children in Families Under Stress. New Directions for Child Development.* San Francisco: Jossey-Bass, 1984, pp. 35–46. As cited in Reid, William J., and Crisafulli, Alida, "Marital Discord and Child Behavior Problems: A Meta-Analysis," *Journal of Abnormal Psychology,* 18:1 (1990), pp. 105–17.

Parker, Douglas A., and Harford, Thomas C., "Alcohol-Related Problems, Marital Disruption and Depressive Symptoms among Adult Children of Alcohol Abusers in the United States," *Journal of Studies on Alcohol,* 49:4 (1989), pp. 306–13.

Peterson, James L., and Zill, Nicholas, "Marital Disruption, Parent-Child Relationships, and Behavior Problems in Children," *Journal of Marriage and the Family,* vol. 48 (May 1986), pp. 295–307.

Porter, Beatrice and O'Leary, K. Daniel, "Marital Discord and childhood behavior problems," *Journal of Abnormal Psychology,* vol. 8 (1980), pp. 287–95. As cited in Demo, David H., and Acock, Alan C., "The Impact of Divorce on Children," *Journal of Marriage and the Family,"* vol. 50 (August 1988), pp. 619–48.

Power, C., and Estaugh, V., "The Role of Family Formation and Dissolution in Shaping Drinking Behavior in Early Adulthood," *British Journal of Addiction,* vol. 85 (1990), pp. 521–30.

Reid, William J., and Crisafulli, Alida, "Marital Discord and Child Behavior Problems: A Meta-Analysis," *Journal of Abnormal Child Psychology,* 18:1 (1990), pp. 105–17.

Rollins, Boyd, and Thomas, Darwin, "Parental Support, Power, and Control Techniques in the Socialization of Children." In: Burr, W.R., et al (eds.), *Contemporary Theories About the Family,* vol. 1. New York: Free Press, 1979, pp. 317–48. As cited in Booth, Alan, "The State of the American Family," *Journal of Family Issues,* 8:4 (December 1987), pp. 429–30.

Rubin, Isaac Theodore, M.D., *The Angry Book.* New York: Collier Books, 1969.

Rutter, M., "Parent-Child Separation: Psychological Effects on the Children," *Journal of Child Psychology and Psychiatry,* vol. 12 (1971), pp. 233–60. As cited in Cama, Kathleen A., and Resnick, Gary, "Styles of Conflict Resolution and Cooperation Between Divorced Parents: Effects on Child Behavior and Adjustment," *American Journal of Orthopsychiatry,* 59: 4 (1989), pp. 560–75.

Sardon, J., *"Evolution de la nupitalite et de la divortialite en Europe dupuis la fin des annees 1960,"* Population, vol. 41, (1986), pp. 463–82. As cited in Martin, Teresa Castro, and Bumpass, Larry L., "Recent Trends in Marital Disruption," *Demography,* 26:1 (February 1989), pp. 37–50.

Stoker, Ann, and Swadi, Harith, "Perceived Family Relationships in Drug Abusing Adolescents," *Drug and Alcohol Dependence,* vol. 25 (1990), pp. 293–97.

Tschann, Jeanne M.; Johnston, Janet R.; Kline, Marsha, and Wallerstein, Judith S., "Family Process and Children's Functioning During Divorce," *Journal of Marriage and the Family,* vol. 51 (May 1989), pp. 431–44.

Turecki, Stanley, and Tonner, Leslie, *The Difficult Child.* New York: Bantam Books, 1985.

Vaughn, Diane *Uncoupling.* New York: Vintage Books, 1968.

Visher, Emily B., and Visher, John S., "Parenting Coalitions After Remarriage: Dynamics and Therapeutic Guidelines," *Family Relations,* vol. 38 (1989), pp. 65–70.

———, "Parenting Coalitions After Remarriage: Dynamics and Therapeutic Guidelines," *Family Relations,* vol. 36 (January 1989), pp. 65–70.

Wallerstein, Judith S., "Children After Divorce: Wounds That Don't Heal," *The Psychiatric Times,* August 1989, pp. 8–11.

———, and Blakeslee, Sandra, *Second Chances.* New York: Ticknor & Fields, 1989.

Woody, Jane D.; Colley, Patrick E.; Schlegelmilch, June; Maginn, Paul, and Balsanek, Judith, "Child Adjustment to Parental Stress Following Divorce," *Social Casework: The Journal of Contemporary Social Work,* September 1984, pp. 405–12.

Zaslow, Martha J., "Sex Differences in Children's Response to Parental Divorce: 1. Research Methodology and Postdivorce Family Forms," *American Journal of Orthopsychiatry,* 58:33 (July 1988), pp. 355–78.

Zill, Nicholas, and Peterson, J., "Marital Disruption and the Child's Need for Psychological Help." Report prepared for NIMH, 1983. As cited in Peterson, James L., and Zills, Nicholas, "Marital Disruption, Parent-Child Relationships, and Behavior Problems in Children," *Journal of Marriage and the Family,* vol. 48 (May 1986), pp. 295–307.

Index

A
Abandonment
  fears of, 36
  feelings of, 31
Acting out, 25, 47, 84-86
  symptoms, 85-86
Adolescent
  developmental stages, 42-44
  developmental tasks, 44-46
  mistakes in dealing with, 48-52
  parents' response to, 103-104
  problems intensified by divorce, 37
  problems precipitated by divorce, 17
  relationship with parent, 103-104
  view of divorce, 105-106
Aggression, in adolescents, 45-46
Alcohol, adolescent use of, 87-88
Ambivalence, about children, 10-11, 25, 104, 111
Anger
  of children, 67, 106
  healthy versus unhealthy, 59-60
  letting go of, 71-72
  managing, 62, 73-74
  at spouse's chemical dependency, 72-73
Angry Book, The (Rubin), 62
Antisocial behavior, in adolescents, 86-87

Anxiety, of children, 26

B
Behavior problems, 17
  see also Acting out; Aggression; Anger; Substance abuse
Biopsychosocial disease model, 78-79
Bipolar disorders, 81
  see also Depression, mental
Blame
  of others, 63
  see also Self-blame

C
Changing school, 31
Chemical dependency
  diagnosis and treatment, 64-65
  as source of marriage strain, 13
  spouse's anger and, 72-73
Children
  as complication of divorce, 9
  as confidants, 35
  divorce and, 9
  maturity overestimated, 15-16, 41, 49
  as source of marriage strain, 11
College education, paying for, 109
College students, emotional disorders, 81

Confidant, child as, 26, 49
Conflict, marital, 60-64
  during long-range phase, 38
  forms of, 69-70
  harmful effects on children, 66-69
  reducing, 55
  rules for managing, 75
Control, issues of marital, 61
Counseling
  for anger, 75
  during long-range phase, 40
  in early disintegration phase, 26-27
  in immediate aftermath phase, 37
  in overt crisis phase, 31-32
  when to seek, 18
  see also Psychotherapy
Custody agreements, 38

D
Date rape, 87-88
Dating
  after divorce, 55, 111-112
  child and, 110
  in immediate aftermath phase, 33-34, 36
Death, versus divorce, 8
Death rate, for adolescents and young adults, 92
Denial
  of adolescent problems, 84
  of marital problems, 23-24
Depression, mental, 81
  clinical stages, 88-89
  in divorced males, 8
  marriage and, 14, 65-66
  substance abuse and, 81
"Difficult" children, 82-83
Difficult Child, The (Turecki), 83
Discipline, 53
  see also Supervision
Dishonesty, 23-24
  see also Denial
Divorce
  adolescent view of, 105-106
  causes, 12-14
  early dissolution phase, 21-26
  immediate aftermath phase, 32-37
  long-range phase, 37-40
  normal versus serious reactions to, 78
  overt crisis phase, 27-32
  parenting role during, 15
  statistics, 5-6, 11
Drug abuse. *See* Chemical dependency; Substance abuse
Dual-diagnosis disorders, 98-99

E
Early dissolution phase
  child's perspective, 24-26
  parent's perspective, 21-24
  scapegoating in, 50
Eating disorders, 17, 67
Embarrassment, divorce as source of, 37
Emotional problems
  of children
  divorce and, 17
  in long-term phase, 39-40
  genetic basis for, 16-17, 79
  risk factors, 79-83
  see also Mental illness
Enabling systems, 79
  chemically dependent and, 83
  during divorce, 84
Ex-spouse, relationship with, 110-111

F
Family history, emotional problems and, 79-80
Family therapy, 94-95
Father
  importance to adolescent, 108
  as single parent, 110
  stress of divorce on, 7-8
Fighting, children's response to, 25-26
Finances
  divorce and, 12
  father's support of child, 109
  managing anger over, 74
  in overt crisis phase, 29
Foundry, The. *See* Regent Hospital

G

Go-between, using child as, 35-36, 68
Grief, for absent parent, 36
Group therapy, 95
Guilt, in overt crisis phase, 28

H

Hospitalization. *See* Inpatient psychiatric treatment
Hostility
  between parents, 21
  see also Fighting
Humor, 74, 75
Hyperactive children. *See* "Difficult" children

I

Idealizing partner, 61
Identity development, in adolescents, 45
Immediate aftermath phase
  children's perspective, 35-37
  parents' perspective, 32-34
Independence, in adolescents, 44-45, 48
Individual therapy, 95
Initiator
  of divorce, 22-24
  in immediate aftermath phase, 33
Inpatient psychiatric treatment, 97-98
Insecurity, marital conflict and, 67

J

Jealousy, at parent's new relationship, 36

L

Learning disorders, in children from divorced families, 82
Long-range phase
  children's perspective, 39-40
  parents' perspective, 37-38
Loss, child's sense of, 30-31

M

Manic depression, 81, 90
Manipulative behavior, 68-69
Marriage
  failure of, 58-59
  strain caused by children, 11
  see also Divorce
Marriage counseling, 93-94
Maturity, of adolescent, 15-16, 41, 49
Mental illness, 80
  divorce as cause in children, 6
  symptoms in adolescents, 90
  see also Mood disorders
Mistrust, 69
Mood disorders, in adolescents, 92
Mother, child's adjustment to divorce and, 107
Moving out, 27-28
  child's response to, 29-30

O

Openness, with children, 54
Overt crisis phase
  children's perspective, 29-32
  parents' perspective, 27-29

P

Parent-adolescent relationship, 48-52, 103-104
Parenting
  during divorce, 15, 52-56, 59
  in early disintegration phase, 22
  in immediate aftermath phase, 34
Part-time parent, 34
Physical changes, in adolescence, 42-43
Problem-solving, styles of, 68
Psychiatric problems. *See* Mental illness
Psychotherapy
  effective, 97
  explained, 93
  see also Therapist

R

Regent Hospital, treatment program, 98-101
Relationships, of adolescents, 46

Remarriage, 111-112
  children and, 34, 36
Resentment lists, 74, 75
Responsibility, parents' abdication of, 49
Reunion fantasies, 36
Rubin, Theodore Isaac, 62

S

Scapegoating, 49-51, 94
School problems, 17
Second Chances (Wallerstein and Blakeslee), 108-109
Secrecy, 25
Self-blame
  of adolescents, 30
  of parents, 10
Sexuality
  in adolescents, 45-46
  appropriate behavior of parents, 55
Single parent
  difficulties of, 34
  father as, 110
  mother as, 8, 107
Somatic complaints, 17
Stress
  divorce as major source of, 7-8
  in early disintegration phase, 22
  family system and, 94
  main sources of, 79
Substance abuse
  and adolescent death rate, 92
  in adolescents, 87-88
  in children of divorce, 13
  depression and, 81
  marriage and, 63-65
Suicidal tendencies, in adolescents, 89
Supervision, importance for children, 110
Support groups, 56
Support. *See* Custody agreements; Finances
Sympathy, 48, 53-54

T

Taking sides, 26
Therapist
  selecting, 96-97
  see also Psychotherapy
Turecki, Stanley, 83

U

Uncoupling (Vaughan), 22

V

Value systems, in adolescents, 46
Vaughan, Diane, 22
Violence, 75
  children and, 67

W

Wallerstein, Judith, 108-109
Withdrawal, 17

Y

Young adults
  developmental tasks, 43-44
  response to parents' divorce, 31
  special problems of parents' divorce, 51-52

From the Founder of Divorce Anonymous

DIVORCE RECOVERY
Healing the Hurt Through Self-Help and Professional Support

by Allan J. Adler, M.D. and Christine Archambault

The psychological, physical, and financial effects of divorce can be overwhelming. Support—either professional or personal—is needed to deal with the pain and confusion of a dissolved relationship.

Learn how to:
- Identify and overcome the fear, anger and guilt of divorce
- Deal with your attorney
- Separate money from emotions
- Avoid legal and financial heartache
- Help your children understand divorce and minimize their pain

ISBN 0-929162-21-8   **Paper, $8.95**

PIA Press, Mail Order Sales
19 Prospect St., Summit, NJ 07902

Please send me _____ copies of Divorce Recovery ($8.95). I am enclosing $_____ . (Please add $1.00 shipping and handling for each book. NJ residents please add appropriate sales tax. Send check or money order—no cash or C.O.D.s please. Allow 6 weeks for delivery.)

Name _____

Address _____

City _____ State _____ Zip _____

Also from Lorraine Henricks

KIDS WHO DO/KIDS WHO DON'T
A Parent's Guide to Teens and Drugs

- 92% of all high school seniors have tried alcohol—4% use it daily.
- 29% of them smoke cigarettes and 30% of kids 12-17 have experimented with an illegal drug.
- While some drug use has leveled off, national surveys show that cocaine use has increased, as have the number of addicted adolescents entering treatment.
- Often parents and families are unwitting accomplices—enablers—in the process that leads teens to drug abuse.

KIDS WHO DO/KIDS WHO DON'T shows you not only what to do if you think your kids are using drugs, but more importantly how your kids can become the kind of kids who don't!

ISBN: 0-929162-11-0 paper $7.95

PIA Press, Mail Order Sales
19 Prospect St., Summit, NJ 07902

Please send me _____ copies of Kids Who Do/Kids Who Don't ($7.95). I am enclosing $_____ . (Please add $1.00 shipping and handling for each book. NJ residents please add appropriate sales tax. Send check or money order—no cash or C.O.D.s please. Allow 6 weeks for delivery.)

Name _____

Address _____

City _____ State _____ Zip _____

Other Books Available

The Good News About Depression, by Mark S. Gold, M.D.
The Good News About Panic, Anxiety and Phobias, by Mark S. Gold, M.D.
Sixty Ways to Make Stress Work For You, by Andrew E. Slaby, M.D., Ph.D., M.P.H.
Guide To The New Medicines Of The Mind, by Irl Extein, M.D., Larry S. Kirstein, M.D., and Peter Herridge, M.D.
The Facts About Drugs and Alcohol, 3rd edition, by Mark S. Gold, M.D.
Get Smart About Weight Control, by Phillip M. Sinaikin, M.D.
High Times/Low Times: The Many Faces of Adolescent Depression, by John E. Meeks, M.D.
On the Edge: The Love/Hate World of the Borderline Personality, by Neil D. Price, M.D.
Overcoming Insomnia, by Donald R. Sweeney, M.D., Ph.D.
Light Up Your Blues: Understanding and Overcoming Seasonal Affective Disorders, by Robert N. Moreines, M.D.
A Parent's Guide to Common and Uncommon School Problems, by David A. Gross, M.D. and Irl L. Extein, M.D.
Psychiatric Skeletons: Tracing the Legacy of Mental Illness In the Family, by Steven D. Targum, M.D.
Life On A Roller Coaster: Coping With the Ups and Downs of Mood Disorders, by Ekkehard Othmer, M.D., Ph.D., and Sieglinde C. Othmer, Ph.D.
A Consumer's Guide to Psychiatric Diagnosis, by Mark A. Gould, M.D.
Aftershock, by Andrew E. Slaby, M.D., Ph.D., M.P.H.
Kids Out of Control, by Alan M. Cohen, M.D.
A Parent's Guide To Teens and Cults, by Larry E. Dumont, M.D. and Richard I. Altesman, M.D.
The Family Contract, by Howard I. Leftin, M.D.
Family Addictions, A Guide For Surviving Alcohol and Drug Abuse, by Charles R. Norris, Jr., M.D.
Kids On the Brink: Understanding the Teen Suicide Epidemic, by David B. Bergman, M.D.
Codependency, Sexuality and Depression, by William E. Thornton, M.D.
When Self-Help Isn't Enough: Overcoming Addiction and Psychiatric Disorders, by A. Scott Winter, M.D.
No More Secrets, No More Shame: Understanding Sexual Abuse and Psychiatric Disorders, by David A. Sack, M.D.
Living with Pain by William S. Makarowski, M.D.
Living with Head Injury: A Guide for Families, by Richard C. Senelick, M.D., and Cathy E. Ryan
Kids Who Do/Kids Who Don't: A Parent's Guide To Teens and Drugs, by Lorraine Henricks, M.D.
Caught In the Crossfire: The Impact of Divorce on Young People, by Lorraine Henricks, M.D.